he Hard Questions that will Lead You to

The *Ah-hah!* Moment

By Fawn Germer

STRAUSS BOOKS

First edition June, 2010

The *Ah-hah!* Moment

Germer, Fawn.
Other titles by Fawn Germer:
Hard Won Wisdom, Perigee Books, 2001
Mustang Sallies, Perigee Books, 2004
Mermaid Mambo, Newhouse Books, 2007
The NEW Woman Rules, Network Books, 2007
Finding the UP in the Downturn, Newhouse Books, 2009
www.fawngermer.com or her blog at www.hardwonwisdom.com.
Speaking information: info@fawngermer.com or (727) 467-0202.
Strauss Books
Printed in the United States of America
ISBN 978-0-9795466-3-1
Library of Congress Control Number: 2010906472

Edited by Lynn Stratton
Copy-Review by Jayne Bray
Interior design by Salah Talhami
Cover design by Steve Peterson
Cover photography by Lisa Presnail

For my precious mother, who dared to fight.

Acknowledgments

As I write this, I am losing my mother. She is the strong, vibrant woman who has never iven up – not even now, as she fades into the thickest fog of Alzheimer's. As my family has nade hard end-of-life decisions with the help of Hospice, Mom has somehow managed to ommunicate a will to live – even though she cannot speak and can barely move. First, after uffering a paralyzing stroke, and later, with the onset of Alzheimer's, Mom faced adversity and found a rich, profound life – filling it with her own truth and love.

At her side is the man I admire most on this earth: my dad, Fred Germer, who has never un from the challenges her 18 years of illness have presented. He gladly embraced his role as her caregiver and still found hope and light in moments when others would see only darkness. I have learned so much from this man's brave love. He has made me strong.

I am so honored to be their daughter.

I wish to thank Julie Hipp, my main support in this world, who has my back at every turn.

nd, thanks to my friends, who have made my life an Ah-Hah! Moment. With them, I discover more wonder and adventure than I ever imagined.

Thanks to my editor, Lynn Stratton, and my second-read editor, Jayne Bray. Without editors, writers are naked in their mistakes. They've kept me fully clothed.

I need to give a shout-out to the Network of Executive Women, the group where I have found several hundred soul mates.

And, finally, thanks to the readers who inspire me to write.

Contents

Introduction **15**
Checking Your Baggage **19**
The Maid and the Millionaire 20
Where's Your Baggage? 22
Personal Inventory 26
Rewriting Your Life's Script **37**
Beginning the Process 40
How to Turn the Negatives into Positives 43
Sometimes, the Bags Are Too Heavy to Lift 44
Which of Your Stories are Doing Damage? 46
How Affirmations Work 49
Things Don't Change Overnight 51
Making the Commitment 54
The Measure of a Winner Comes from Within 55
Realizing What You Already Have 60
EXERCISE: Going Back to the Beginning 61
Confused About Your Purpose in Life? It's Simple. 67
Letting Go of Your Need for Control **71**
You Don't Want Your Life Micromanaged,
So Why Are You Micromanaging Others? 72
You Choose Your Micromanagers 76
Life is Simply an Out-of-Control Experience 80
Controlling Your Control Issues 85
Let Go, Let God 86
Set Goals That You Can "Control" 88
Affirmations to Begin Your Change Process 91
Deciding to Decide **93**
Your Role as a Decision Maker 94
What's the Problem? 97
What are your options? 102
Assess the risk 103
Leave Your Bubble 105
Getting Input That Counts 107
What if? 108
Decide! No, WAIT! 109
Don't Be Impulsive 110
Decide Not to Decide 112
The Weighted Decision Table 113
You Can Handle the Consequences 114
Get on with it 114
Deciding to Decide 116
Decision Checklist 118

It's NOT About Balance. It's About Choices. 121
Are You Making the Right Choices? 123
Checking in With Yourself. 126
Housework Can Be Delegated. Life Can't. 128
What Matters Most? 129
Go Ahead. Just Drop the Ball. 132
Evaluating Your Time Drains 132
Conscious Scheduling 134
Balancing Your Life. 137
The Firewall Between Your Time and Theirs 138
How Do You Do all of That and Raise a Family? 139
Stop Feeling Selfish. It is YOUR Life. 143
When You Have Too Much To Do and No Time To Do It. 147
It's Only Stuff 151
Live NOW, Not Later 157
Ten Minutes of Mindfulness 162
What's Wrong With Our Attention Spans? 163
EXERCISE: Breathe in. Breathe out. 165
EXERCISE: One Thing at a Time 166
EXERCISE: Eat Less. Enjoy it More. 167
EXERCISE: Go Outside and Take a Look Around.. 168
Finally, Live NOW, Not Later 168
Don't Force the Universe. Listen to it. 173
Ten Steps Out of Tough Times and Into Life Transition 175
Get Out of Your Own Way 179
EXERCISE: Taking Stock. 182
EXERCISE: Fifteen Minute Reality Check 187
Get a Grip 192
Volunteer. Do Good Things. 197
Trust Your Instincts 201
What holds us back?. 206
Can You Leave the Group? 209
Finally Taking My Power 211
Peace Within 215

Introduction

You'll learn pretty quickly that, even though I make my living as a motivational speaker who writes self-help books, I can't stand most motivational speakers who write self-help books. There is an underlying current of phoniness in them that I find, well, repulsive.

I once saw a speaker telling people experiencing brutal financial hardship that all they needed to do was plunk down $379 for her financial wealth system, and that would cure everything. But, they had to act within two hours, because if they left the conference without anteing up, the price would double. I saw another speaker who promised multimillionaire-style wealth from his insights into multi-level marketing for (I couldn't believe it) $10,000. If that kind of money was an issue, he said, no worries: he accepted credit cards, but they could always get an equity line of credit, and take money out of their homes to cover his charges. A reporter once told me about a friend of hers who is making millions teaching others to simplify their lives, yet her life is filled with mansions and minks.

I go to some of these events and see slick people with slick voices offering slick solutions and I cringe. I'm not slick. I'm someone who has faced obstacles, persevered and learned that life is a brilliant experience of light and hope – if that is what we choose for it to be. It's a big deal for me to publicly say that I believe in the Law of Attraction and the power of affirmations because I was one of the world's greatest skeptics. I spent most of my career working as a hard-edged investigative reporter who was pointedly cynical and naturally negative. I always dismissed any new age / self-help / pop psychology concepts as woo-woo garbage.

My skepticism about the self-help world was based largely on a lack of credentials for the people touting their magic solutions. I am not a psychologist, but I have interviewed hundreds of the most accomplished leaders and trailblazers of our times to find out what they learned the hard way. I've talked to everyone from Hillary Clinton, Martina Navratilova and Susan Sarandon to Nobel Peace Prize winners, Olympic athletes, spiritual leaders, Academy Award winners, scientists, presidents, prime ministers, CEOs, Indian chiefs and more. I have a perspective that others don't have. I've often said that every time I write a book, it's like I get a million dollars worth of free therapy, and it's the truth. Sometimes, I learn by what has made others successful. Sometimes, I learn from what has held them back. The important thing is, I learn. I keep growing. And I never stop trying.

A million years ago, I asked my then-husband if he'd like to go out for dinner with the girls. "Naw," he said. "You all go out and talk about things like 'growth.'" I still laugh about that because that is something that separates a lot of men and women. Women are prone to self-evaluate and ponder where they are and where they are going. Often, we over-analyze to a fault. Some men do that too, of course, but women do look at themselves in a way that can either be hypercritical or hyper-helpful. It's good to know where you've been, how far you've come and where you plan to go. But don't over-analyze to the point that you begin playing new and powerful negative tapes inside your head that remind you of where you have fallen short. Just look at how you have grown and evolved over the years.

If you have grown into the kind of individual you admire, you've won the game. If you don't admire who you are, you can do two things to right your course: first, change what you need to change, and second, let go of the regret, guilt and negativity that you have felt about your shortcomings. Again, remember that you *are* growing. If you haven't done it yet, now is the time to take charge of your growth process and accept responsibility for the individual you are.

The techniques in this workbook have changed my perspective and made me successful in life. I am truly happy. My life has meaning. I don't slide into negativity and I enjoy every minute of my day. It's not about making a living, but making a life. I am an imperfect person who lives what is, for me, a perfect life. That's because I have made peace with my imperfections and, even better, have come to embrace them. I don't have to be the smartest person in the room, or the most attractive. I don't have to be the best housekeeper or bring home the biggest paycheck. I just have to live a beautiful life, and that means dis-entangling myself from the negative influences that have brought me sadness or difficulties in the past. I've had to make my own changes, re-writing my self-talk, controlling my consumption of negative news and eliminating negative people from my life.

Every one of us has our share of dysfunction in our families, relationships, careers, and perspective. Big deal. We can fixate on the negative or get on with living. I choose living. The choice is yours. It is *absolutely* yours. Do you want to be happy? Then be happy. Do you want to be miserable? Then be miserable. You aren't condemned to misery in this life, but you are forced to cope and adapt. That comes down to developing an inner fortitude and confidence that gives you the certainty that you are strong enough to deal with whatever life throws your way. Don't seek an easy life, seek the strength to handle whatever comes.

Deep within you, you already have all the answers. You just haven't been asking the right questions.

Checking Your Baggage

I was in my 20s the first time I heard someone talk about "people with baggage." Those were people with issues that kept them from functioning at their best in relationships or at work. Since I had a loving and rather uneventful childhood, I thought how wonderful it was that I was not a person with baggage.

Decades later, I've got baggage. We all do. The more we interact with other people and experience the dramas that come our way, the more we have opportunities to get banged up, to win, lose, love, divorce, and so on. I've got baggage from relationships that didn't work. I've got baggage from bad bosses I didn't like. I've even got baggage from failed diets. I've got baggage from hard lessons learned along the way.

That's just fine, as long as I check my baggage and continue to live a joyful life. The problem comes when people can't check their baggage and get on with their lives. Instead of learning from life's hardships, they drag their baggage around wherever they go. They can't let their heart heal after it has been broken. They can't hold their heads up after they've been fired. They keep their wounds open for years, rather than learning, healing and getting on with life.

There are happy people in this world and there are unhappy people in this world. Somewhere along the way, they made the choice to be one or the other.

My life is not without heartache or stress. I have openly shared professional setbacks that came my way, but I've also had my share of relationships that didn't work, and I have experienced the immense pain that comes from a sick parent who has suffered tremendously for nearly two decades. I've also got a sibling issue that is painful and intense. But, for all of these difficulties, I am the happiest person I know.

I decided to live a happy life. I decided to define myself by the joy I could experience with every fresh new day, rather than letting myself be pulled down by the things that did not turn out the way I would have liked. Rather than getting sucked into a vortex of negativity, I programmed myself to live with a "big picture" perspective that offered me joy, hope and perspective.

You can be happy – or not. It is your choice.

The Maid and the Millionaire

Several years ago, I met a very wealthy man who would change my life. He hired me to be his writing coach and paid me a lot as we argued endlessly about the book he wanted to write. It was such a brother/sister tug-of-war, and it meant a lot to me. Our professional relationship stretched over four years as he continued to write and rewrite his book.

After we concluded our working relationship, we maintained a close friendship, and throughout the years, I watched him slowly destroy himself with alcohol. He'd been in rehab four times, and I knew it would only be a matter of time before the alcohol would kill him. What I didn't know was that it would do something worse.

One day, he drank so much that he tumbled down to the bottom of the stairs in his magnificent home. He suffered a brain bleed so severe that it pushed one half of his brain to the other side. His kidneys stopped functioning. His lungs collapsed. He was paralyzed.

At first, we were told to brace for his death, but he lived. Two years later, he is the youngest person in an assisted living center, unable to care for himself or come and go without aid. He uses a walker or a wheelchair. He can't go to the bathroom without help.

This is the tragic final chapter of the life of a maverick businessman who made millions before retiring young. He'd had a hard childhood, raised in poverty and constantly beaten by an alcoholic father who eventually shot and killed himself. With that in his emotional DNA, it is surprising that my friend was able to become one of America's most successful businessmen in the dot.com era. But he knew how to rock and roll a sales force and he did it with a global reach, taking home millions in his paycheck.

All those millions in the bank, yet he was the saddest, loneliest man I have ever known. He just wanted to be loved and appreciated. People saw that and conned him out of most of his money. The beautiful young woman whom he'd been involved with for many years had been stringing him along – getting more than a million dollars of his money without spending more than a couple of days a year with him. When she was told what happened to him and that her money supply was cut off, she did not fly out to be with him, she did not call him and she never sent a card.

I learned a life-changing lesson from him years ago when he and I went to a conference, then stayed over to work on his book. The housekeeper came into his room and my client gave her $20 and told her he wouldn't be needing any maid service.

She smiled broadly and said, "Thank you so much! I take all of these tips and give them to my church." I saw emotions in her eyes that I have never seen in his. Peace. Certainty. Fulfillment.

I never forgot that. On paper, that housekeeper had nothing. But, she really had everything.

She had everything and he had nothing. And now he continues to struggle to live and it makes me so sad because he never knew the joy that poor woman had in her heart.

This taught me what those millions of dollars were worth. They did not buy him peace of mind about his past. He admitted to me that his self-esteem was terrible, that he'd try to buy love with money – and that didn't work. He had so many resources that he couldn't hit rock bottom.

It is such a dark story, but it really shows how money does not buy happiness. News articles and books that lauded his business genius did not bring him joy. Six homes that he proclaimed "architectural masterpieces" did not make him happy. The beautiful girlfriend didn't do it.

Happiness is within. It is free. You just have to open yourself up to it.

I have often said that we have the same amount of happiness available to us regardless of our social class, but I do add one caveat – as long as our survival and safety are ensured. I don't think a person without resources who is living on the streets and fearing for his or her life has the same happiness available that I have.

Life is fragile. Love what you have, because once you enter a realm of gratitude, you suddenly realize that you already have enough. You just have to appreciate it.

Where's Your Baggage?

The following checklist lets you know where your issues are and which thoughts are holding you back.

Baggage Checklist	Always	Usually	Sometimes	Rarely	Never
I live every day to the fullest.					
I eat the right, healthy foods.					
I weigh what I should.					
Other people "get" and appreciate me.					
I am liked by other people.					
I am respected by other people.					
I like the person I have grown up to be.					
I leave the past behind me.					
I am smart and competent.					
I like how I look.					
I have good romantic relationships.					
I have good friendships.					
I am as focused and driven as I think I should be.					
I have a strong spiritual connection.					
I am appreciated by my family.					
I have enough time to enjoy my life.					
I do a good job of prioritizing what matters – and I honor those priorities.					
I make prudent financial decisions.					
I am financially stable.					
I am aware of my "issues" and deal with them.					
I forgive myself for mistakes I have made in the past.					
I confront my problems directly.					
Life has been fair to me.					
I feel successful at life.					

Baggage Checklist	Always	Usually	Sometimes	Rarely	Never
I feel good about the life balance choices I make.					
I feel young.					
I act young.					
I embrace getting older.					
I am happy and upbeat.					
I am proud of myself.					
I am proud of where I live.					
I like having visitors to my home.					
I have good self-esteem.					
I have strong self-confidence.					
I feel I can take care of myself.					
I am a good housekeeper.					
I am a good spouse or partner. (If applicable.)					
I am a good parent. (If applicable.)					
I am a good daughter or son. (If applicable.)					
I am a good neighbor.					
I am a good citizen.					
I am a good human being.					
I am a nice person.					
I do kind things for others without expecting anything in return.					
I have a pleasant personality.					
My childhood memories are generally good.					
I felt safe as a child.					
I felt loved as a child.					
I was proud of my mother.					

Baggage Checklist	Always	Usually	Sometimes	Rarely	Never
I was proud of my father.					
I was proud of my sibling(s).					
I was proud of the home I lived in as a child.					
I trusted my mother.					
I trusted my father.					
I trusted my siblings.					
I believe I deserve my professional success.					
I believe I deserve the comforts that I have in my life.					
I believe I deserve the respect of others.					
I am open and truthful about who I am.					
People see the real me.					
I feel that I have lived up to my potential.					
I seize opportunity whenever I can.					
I make choices that take care of my health.					
I have fun.					
I have time for myself.					
I believe I have a great future ahead of me.					
I feel that I am in control.					
I get as much as I give in relationships.					
I was emotionally abused as a child.					
I was physically abused as a child.					
I was sexually abused as a child.					
I was emotionally abused in adult relationships.					
I was physically abused in adult relationships.					
I was sexually abused in adult relationships.					

Baggage Checklist	Always	Usually	Sometimes	Rarely	Never
Other people think I am more confident than I really am.					
There are things I do not feel comfortable disclosing here that impact my confidence and happiness.					
My secrets are powerful.					

Now, let's go deeper.

Personal Inventory

Evaluating my self-esteem when I was a child from 1 to 8 years old:

- I felt good about myself because…

- I felt bad about myself because…

Evaluating my self-esteem from age 9 to 12:

- I felt good about myself because…

- I felt bad about myself because…

Evaluating my self-esteem from age 13 to 16:

- I felt good about myself because…

- I felt bad about myself because…

Evaluating my self-esteem from age 17 to 20:

- I felt good about myself because…

- I felt bad about myself because…

Evaluating my self-esteem from age 20 to 30:

- I felt good about myself because…

- I felt bad about myself because…

Evaluating my self-esteem from age 30 to 40:

- I felt good about myself because…

- I felt bad about myself because…

Evaluating my self-esteem from age 40 to 50:

- I felt good about myself because…

- I felt bad about myself because…

Evaluating my self-esteem from age 50 to 60:

- I felt good about myself because...

- I felt bad about myself because...

Evaluating my self-esteem over age 60:

- I felt good about myself because...

- I felt bad about myself because...

Evaluating my self esteem RIGHT NOW:

- I feel good about myself because...

- I feel bad about myself because...

The most consistent sources of sadness and anxiety of my life have been…

1.

2.

3.

If I could change three things about myself, they would be:

1.

2.

3.

If I could change three things about my childhood, they would be:

1.

2.

3.

If I could change three things about my professional history, they would be:

1.

2.

3.

The happiest time of my life was when:

The three things I would celebrate most about the way my life is going right now are:

1.

2.

3.

Three things I would change are:

1.

2.

3.

4.

The reasons I don't make the changes I should make in order to live a happier life are:

The most positive forces in my life are:

The most negative forces in my life are:

I eliminate exposure to negative forces by:

Here is what I need to accomplish in my lifetime in order to feel "successful":

The three traits I admire most about myself are:

1.

2.

3.

The three traits I admire least about myself are:

1.

2.

3.

Other people like me because:

Other people dislike me because:

If I worry about what others think of me, it's because:

This affects my life by:

On any given day, on a scale of 1 to 10 with 10 being highest, my average happiness score is:

I feel guilty about:

I am embarrassed because:

The previous two exercises are designed to get you to go deep to see how you are getting in your own way. We all have our "trigger" issues that hold us back, and the exercises should help you to clearly identify where yours are. As you review your answers, ask yourself a few questions.

1. Do I need to let these issues make me feel bad about myself?

2. Will they matter when I am living my last day on earth?

3. How much time and energy am I losing in order to worry about these things?

4. Have I blown these issues out of proportion?

5. Can I decide not to worry about these matters for 24 hours and honor that decision? If so, can I go a whole week? Even longer?

Rewriting Your Life's Script

You can spend thousands of dollars and many years in therapy trying to figure out the roots of your insecurities and how they have affected your life. Or, you can look at how you have answered the questions in the previous chapter and see what you can do to take charge of your thoughts, re-write your negative scripts and get on with living a full life unencumbered by baggage.

This isn't easy – but it also isn't as hard as you might think. By looking within and literally re-writing your negative scripts, you take a powerful first step. Then, go one step further: Write new affirmations that will help you turn your new life script into the one that plays automatically in your head.

We are always talking to ourselves. We wake up in the morning and get ready for the day and decide quickly whether it is a good hair day or a bad hair day, whether we look fat or thin. For some reason, we are very eager to self-criticize. We do it all the time. Why? What possible good can come from that? Yet, we invite self-negativity and give it unlimited air time in our brains. We will freely subject ourselves to a powerful barrage of nastiness, yet we'd never be so cruel to a stranger, or even to someone we don't like. We are mean to ourselves, and we don't even see it for what it is.

Think about the negative things you have said to yourself in the last 24 hours. Just think of them! If someone said those things to your child, you'd want to rip that person apart. Yet, *you* are saying those terrible things to yourself, the one person you must love above all others! Why do you stand for it? Do you realize that the tapes are rolling when you do this? That those negative thoughts and feelings get stored on your internal hard drive? That they limit you in every possible way?

It's time for an intervention. If you want a better life, you must take the easiest of baby steps to make it happen. All you have to do is figure out a few good things to say to yourself in order to get your mind to let go of the negativity.

I know the cynics will just roll their eyes and walk away at the mere suggestion of using affirmations to refocus and re-energize their lives, and that is fine. It's their own choice to limit themselves.

Countless studies have proven the connection between positive affirmations (either through self-talk or hypnosis) and positive results. The concept is this: If you tell yourself you are attractive and fun to be around enough times, your brain will overwrite your negative tapes that say you are unattractive and unworthy. You will actually believe it if you say it enough times.

It works. Let's just say I am in one of my disorganized spells. I might say to myself, "I'm a mess. I can't get anything done, my desk is out of control and I can't focus." Well, what is the result? I can't get anything done and I can't focus. But I can also launch into affirmation mode and repeat, "I am getting more organized by the minute. I am on task and producing better than ever." I might say it fifty times the first day, thirty times the second day, and so on. It doesn't take long for me to shift into high gear and start focusing hard and doing my work.

If you have your doubts about this positive self-talk programming, take a minute to examine what your negative self-talk has accomplished. I am sure it is significant.

Unfortunately, we humans are really mean to ourselves. We berate ourselves for gaining weight, failing in relationships, struggling at work, getting into tussles with family, not doing enough for our kids. We refuse to let go of the inevitable criticism that comes our way through the years, remembering a kind word of praise for five minutes but a passing swipe until we die. We fixate on the few people who don't like us, rather than the many who do. The list of sour thoughts that we put in our head and keep there goes on and on and on.

And, since we are sensitive beings, we don't just acknowledge our shortcomings, we revisit them again and again and again. We remind ourselves how we fall short – and we aren't even consciously doing it. We cling to nasty remarks that may have been said about us years ago – even decades ago – as though they were true and permanent. We joke about ourselves to others, but while those self-deprecating put-downs may be humorous, they serve to re-enforce our negative self-image.

And when it comes to body image? For my other books, I interviewed world renowned leaders who acknowledged their horrible self-esteem problems that were rooted in what they weighed or how they looked. Few even tried to pretend their self-esteem was rock solid. This is the disease of our generation: We beat ourselves up.

If we've failed at something, we remind ourselves of it long after we should have moved on. We tell ourselves we aren't smart enough or fast enough or savvy enough to try something especially hard or new.

This is how we have *programmed* our thinking. We have put all those dark thoughts in our heads and repeated them so many times that they are the first thoughts we have when it comes to our performance, our place in the world and our self-worth. Write down ten negative things you have told yourself this week, and really look at them. Are they grounded in reality? Would other people say those things about you? Would they say it with such vitriol? Besides, you are a flawed individual – just like everybody else. Perfectly flawed, and that is okay.

So, don't be so skeptical of the value of positive self-talk until you really look at the power and influence of all the negative self-talk with which you've filled your brain. Yes, isn't it a wonder how some of us voluntarily build ourselves up to be worthless, unattractive failures?

If you look in the mirror and see "fat," you will be fat. If you look at your career track and think "average," you will be average. If you look at possibility and see impossibility, you will encounter impossibility. You know it's true that when you say you can't, you can't.

So this book will, in part, teach you how to believe you can, because you can.

The beauty of it is, it is not hard at all to erase those negative tapes and overwrite them with positive ones that will drive you to a less stressful, more productive and happier life.

Beginning the Process

We all have a story about ourselves, and usually, it's really powerful fiction. There was a time in my life when one of my stories was that I would spend my golden years old, sick, broke and alone. Someone stopped me and said, "Why are you telling yourself that story?" I didn't have an answer. There is no reason I should have been thinking that. The "broke" idea was born when my stocks took a serious nosedive in the dot.com era. The "sick" idea came because my mother had a major stroke that paralyzed her when she was just 66. The "alone" idea came because I didn't have children and wasn't in a relationship at the time. I added it all together and figured the old/sick/broke/alone storyline was mine.

But my friend really pushed me to change that storyline, and I did – almost instantly. I bought my first investment property. I came up with a new strategy for my money. And

I decided I would be healthy in my golden years because I am fit and strong. Now my golden years story is: "Old, active, comfortable and secure."

That is an example of rewriting a negative life script. We have so many stories that we tell about our lives, and they do a lot of damage – even when they are true.

A few years ago, an extremely successful professional woman named Elaine discovered her 80-year-old father's 40-year-old second wife had drained almost all of the family money out of her father's accounts. Her father did not see the problem because he thought his wife Alicia was a good businesswoman who had his best interests at heart. Elaine knew better, and confronted her. Alicia's response was to convince Elaine's dad that his daughter was ruthless and greedy, and cared more about his money than him. He firmly told Elaine that she'd either have to accept and love Alicia or lose her relationship with him. She continued to visit him, but she was in anguish and her resentment soured their relationship.

For two years, Elaine wallowed in pain and bitterness. She felt betrayed, rejected and victimized. She talked about it – endlessly. Finally, she realized that her suffering wasn't doing anything to fix the situation. It was punishing *her.*

Since she couldn't fix the situation, what could she do to help herself move on from it?

I told her she could rewrite the script.

This powerful technique combines the science of affirmations with your own personal insights in order to turn dark into light. It works. And, it saves you a fortune in therapy bills.

She sat down for two hours and rewrote the story she'd been telling herself. Here is a small part of what she wrote:

"It is now that I say, enough – and make the decision to believe it. I am taking my life back for myself, because I have missed so much by worrying about things I can't control or change. No, I do not have a perfect father. But I grew up with a father who did love me and teach me. Through his lessons, I was given the confidence to be a strong, vibrant and successful woman. He gave me the tools to take care of myself. I grew up safe. I was never abused and was always loved…

"My father has tried so hard to be a good father. He just lacked the backbone to go up against Alicia. Theirs is a relationship that I do not comprehend, and it is one that has caused me to suffer and experience loss and heartache. But today I make the decision to rebuild my relationship with my father by letting go of my anger over money. Instead of trying to change what I can't change, I choose now to celebrate what is good and powerful. I have made peace with Alicia because she makes my father happy and I want him in my life."

This script went on for a few pages, and closed with affirmations:

> *"I accept and return my father's love without condition.*
>
> *If I had to choose between the dollars Alicia has taken or the tools my father gave me to confidently stand on my own, I would take the tools every time.*
>
> *I am grateful that God gave me a father who believed in me, supported me and gave me the tools to be successful.*
>
> *I am deeply loved by my father. I love him back – without condition.*
>
> *There is no need for forgiveness because I choose to focus on the love and support he has always given me. Nothing else matters.*

I feel love and joy and have let go of all anger and resentment.

I am the luckiest woman alive, and I thank God for all of my blessings – beginning with my wonderful father.

I only worry about the things I can control."

After we finished writing the script and affirmations, Elaine wondered how she could ever come to absorb and believe the new self-talk. I had her record what she'd written onto her computer, repeating the affirmations four times during the recording. She then burned that recording to a CD and played it in her car nonstop for two weeks. Here is what she said it accomplished:

"It was a miracle. About three days into it, I felt lighter. I'd probably played it fifty times. I'd let go of my anger and felt close to my father again. The whole situation with Alicia lost its energy. It's been a year since I did that and I can truly say that I haven't had a single dark moment since I made the decision to rewrite the story and learn the new script.

"The drama had consumed me, but suddenly, it didn't matter. This was such a gift. I just wish I'd done it two years earlier."

How to Turn the Negatives into Positives

This is where your work gets hard. It's one thing for me to ask you to go deep and explore the issues and events that are holding you back. It's another thing to assign you to rewrite the negatives into productive narratives that will help you to cope and live a less stressful life. This is especially tough when you are dealing with issues that are traumatic.

Sometimes, the Bags Are Too Heavy to Lift

I was just blogging about the death of Wilma Mankiller, the first woman to be elected chief of the Cherokee Nation. She was just 64 and died of pancreatic cancer. Throughout her life, she faced unbelievable adversity, surviving a terrible car accident that forced her to undergo dozens of operations, a neuromuscular disease and a kidney transplant.

I interviewed her for my first book, *Hard Won Wisdom*. She shared insights into her approach to life that showed me that she was automatically writing her life script to be productive for her.

"The biggest challenge in my life has been to try to continue with my life and my work while dealing with an unbelievable array of health issues. I've dealt with that the same way I dealt with the opposition I had because I was a woman. It's a problem, I acknowledge it and I try to deal with it the best way I know how, and then move on. Just like I don't let my energy be siphoned off into questions of whether women should be in leadership, I won't let my energy be siphoned off by a question of health. I can control my mind when I don't control my body. I can do what I can to keep myself well and continue on. It's really a choice. You can dwell on hard or bad things if you want. You don't have to."

You can see what she told herself:

1. True, she had huge setbacks.

2. They weren't going to hold her back.

3. She was still in charge.

Those are the "talking points" that put her on a positive life course, regardless of the negative things that were happening.

With more than 20 years in the newspaper business, I got a front row seat on how ugly life can get. I have met people with stories so horrific that I can't believe the evil some humans are capable of inflicting on others.

My own father immigrated to this country from Germany during the Holocaust after my grandmother took the few pieces of jewelry she saved for herself to bribe the Nazis and free my grandfather from a concentration camp. Dad's once-wealthy family arrived in America completely impoverished, but they rose above it.

His "talking points" have always been:

1. I am so lucky to be in this country and have the opportunities I have.

2. I live in the present, not in the past.

3. I have a beautiful family, a beautiful home and a beautiful life. I am blessed and I am grateful.

His positive approach has served him well. At age 83, he is still a practicing pharmacist. My mother, who has been the love of his life since they married in 1953, is in the cruel, final stages of Alzheimer's Disease as I write this. Dad cared for her at home until it became physically impossible. The day she went to the nursing home, he changed his routine so he could visit her four times a day. It has been a slow, draining goodbye. Yet he calls me every day to report that Mom opened her eyes, she seems to be doing well and (I can hear the tone of his voice lift with happiness and hope) she's alive! Those are his talking points in a situation that others would find completely hopeless. He finds happiness because he lets himself feel love.

It would be absurd for me to think you can tell anyone who has suffered terrible trauma "Don't worry, be happy." But it is amazing how some people surmount the insurmountable and overcome abuse or violence or health challenges or financial disasters and emerge happy – while others facing similar challenges are emotionally crippled for life. Some people are blessed with superhuman fortitude. Others do the best they can to keep on living. Some slide into depression and never recover.

I do think that there is a degree of "choice" when it comes to coping. It amazes me how often one person experiencing a set of circumstances recovers emotionally and another experiencing the same set of circumstances doesn't. There does seem to be real power in knowing that every morning is the start of a fresh new day. You can pick up your baggage and carry it with you, or you can make the choice to live in the glory of a fresh, new moment.

I bring all of this up because I don't want to be so Pollyanna-ish as to say we all have the same bite at the happiness apple. We don't. Some people have much harder challenges, and I wish them every possible source of hope and love. Sometimes, it is much harder to "check" your baggage. Sometimes, it is too hard. Regardless, the challenges of others do serve to remind the rest of us that we don't have it as bad as we think we do. We should be happy.

We have the power to control a great deal when we begin to rewrite our life's script.

Which of Your Stories are Doing Damage?

We all have stories that hold us back. Which one do you want to rewrite first?

Write down a summary of the story you've been telling yourself.

How has this story hurt you?

Take some time to come up with the three to five "talking points" of your new version of the story.

What are the five positive things you can say that will reframe your experience?

Now write your new story. The long version – not the short one.

What do you want to feel after you have accepted this new script into your subconscious?

Now we switch to the second tool in the rewriting process: affirmations.

How Affirmations Work

The concept is very, very simple:

1. If you say something to yourself enough times, you will believe it.

2. If you write it down, it becomes real to your mind.

The downside is just as simple:

1. When you stop repeating those affirmations, they stop working.

2. When they stop working, the most strongly embedded thoughts come back, and since you've been negative much longer than you've been positive, it's the negative thoughts that will come back.

That means:

1. You have to be motivated enough to affirm yourself.

2. And you have to do it, even when you don't feel like it.

Sometimes, it's not so easy. Seriously, repeating ten affirmations five times a day will take you, what, maybe two or three minutes total? But when you are depressed and need self-affirming statements the most, finding the energy to spend those few minutes can be a real challenge.

The tapes inside your head are powerful. If you repeat a negative remark enough times, it will load itself onto the permanent memory on your personal internal hard drive. I don't believe you have the power to completely erase those tapes because it does seem like they are ready to play themselves again as soon as you stop repeating your revised versions through affirmations. But, you have great control over the tapes and possess the ability to keep rewriting over the bad ones, recording positive, constructive and productive affirmations that your psyche will absorb and use if you repeat them often enough.

The key here is, AFFIRMATIONS MUST BE POSITIVE TO WORK. You don't say, "I no longer like to eat junk food." You say, "I love healthy food."

Instead of saying, "I no longer feel bad about my divorce," you say, "I feel good about my divorce because it freed me to enjoy a wonderful new independent life."

Don't say, "I don't speed when I am driving." Say, "I observe the speed limit when I'm driving."

The subconscious works much better with positive information.

But, you have to repeat it, and sometimes, that is the tough part. When you are feeling down, it can be really hard to get yourself into the mindset to spend a few minutes repeating positive affirmations. But they work! So, how do you get yourself to affirm yourself when you don't feel like it?

Just make up your mind that it is time to start feeling better. You want an easier way to live? You can have it, and now is the time to start.

Things Don't Change Overnight

Remember, this is just the start. You don't lose fifty pounds in two weeks; you lose them one pound at a time. You don't begin a fitness regimen by running a marathon; you run a mile or two.

So don't look at the prospect of de-stressing and re-building your life by expecting to change everything by midnight tonight. It's too intimidating. You are who you are. You may want changes, but those changes can't – and won't – happen in an instant.

The one thing I have seen repeatedly in people who face daunting challenges is that they often won't try because the situation seems too big and hard to conquer. They think they must do it all and fix it all – at once, and that's too hard so they just don't bother and they settle for the status quo.

I once had an editor who went on a diet. And gave up smoking. And stopped drinking alcohol. And gave up coffee.

ALL AT ONCE!

Now, there might be one or two hearty sorts who might be able to handle that much life overhaul at once, but not many. Certainly not that editor, who morphed into the meanest, nastiest, foulest co-worker I have ever encountered. Within days, people were *begging* her to embrace her vices again – at least one or two of them.

And, of course, she did. She embraced them all. With fervor.

Twenty years later, she is still embracing them. Although I think she mentioned a few months back that she'd quit smoking.

The lesson here is that you have to mentally and physically position yourself for success, not failure. Even though I encourage you to test and push your limits as far as your imagination will let them, you still must do a reality gut-check. You are a human being who can do only so much at once. Maybe you are the one-in-a-million mastermind who can leap tall buildings in a single bound, but if you can't, you might smash into the wall and give up altogether.

Really look at what you are up against and split the challenges into stages that you can knock off one or two at a time. I know, you're asking how you can dream huge dreams while still grounding yourself within your own human limits. Sounds like quite a contradiction, but it's not. What I am suggesting is that you dream huge dreams, but pace yourself.

Make the decision – *really* make the decision, and make those goals become reality. Once you have some momentum, add to your list. Do more. And then more. The more you do, the more you will be able to do at one time.

Don't fool yourself into thinking you have such superhuman stamina, willpower and determination that you can accomplish everything at once. At the same time, don't use that reality to talk yourself out of striving for goals that seem out of reach. Again, it's pacing. Set a course for yourself that will push you and make you stretch, but don't set one that will kill you.

Pace yourself.

I once interviewed a man at a college graduation who had started his studies back when he was a young father. It had taken him ten years to get that bachelor's degree, and he did it one class at a time. It didn't matter what was going on in his life, he always had one class in progress to move him forward toward his ultimate goal. And he achieved it.

You don't have to fix everything in one day. If you think you do, you will be tempted not to fix anything. Just take small steps.

I travel a lot for my speaking business and the thing I hate most is coming home to a dining room table covered with stacks of mail. I just can't deal with it, and so I leave it. Then the pile grows. And grows.

There came a point where there was not a single inch of space available on that table. One morning, I complained about this to a friend, who told me, "Just set your timer and give it ten minutes of straightening time. You can do the same thing tomorrow. But you only have to do it for ten minutes." Well, that didn't seem so bad, so I told myself I would do it.

I kept putting it off. Noon came and went, two o'clock, four o'clock, and finally I said to myself, "This is ridiculous. It's only ten minutes." So, I set the clock, and focused on that table. Ten minutes later, I realized I was almost finished clearing that table. It only would take another five minutes, which I gladly did. Suddenly, that table was 100 percent clear of clutter.

It is exactly the same when trying to clear the clutter you have stacked up in your brain. Even if the outcome is peace of mind, inner strength and outright joy, the idea of changing your entire thought pattern, perceptions and attitudes sounds like work.

You don't have to change everything today.

You don't have to go into some twenty-three hour Zen zone of affirmation, affirmation, affirmation to reprogram every negative thing about yourself.

Just give it ten minutes.

Just start.

Making the Commitment

The brain makes it easy for us to reprogram our negative tapes and rewrite the stories that hold us down. All it takes is time, concentration and commitment.

How long does it take to rewrite the story and write your affirmations? A couple of hours. You can concentrate for that long.

But it won't work if you aren't committed to the process.

Do you really want to improve your situation?

Are you committed to rewriting your story and writing your affirmations?

Are you committed to repeating your new story script every day for the next two weeks?

Are you committed to repeating your affirmations at least five times a day the first week, three times a day the second week and two times a day the third week?

If you start repeating your old story script, will you go through this process again?

Why do you want to make these changes?

What are you afraid of?

Have you taken responsibility for your own happiness in the past?

Will you take responsibility for your happiness now?

The Measure of a Winner Comes from Within

Sometimes, you just need to lighten up on yourself. Often, the baggage we carry is heavy because we've packed it heavy.

I want to tell you the story of a man I know who is 46 years old, handsome, educated, politically astute, creative and absolutely brilliant. He is also underemployed.

I recently had lunch with him and, once again, I heard him express disappointment that he hasn't accomplished more with his life. He has tried so hard for so many years to get a great job, but it hasn't happened. He's working for $9.75 an hour in retail, in a job with no benefits and no future.

Everything he says about himself is negative. He's too old to compete. His friends have accomplished so much. He's "never done anything" with his life.

It makes me so sad, because I know how hard this guy has tried. He's been trying for years, always sending out more resumes, but never getting the big break he needs.

I suggest that he work harder at networking, but he's truly shy and I know that he won't. I know his introversion costs him plenty in the job market, because people hire people they know. It's the American way. It's reality. But he doesn't mingle.

So, he keeps sending in applications, and he keeps waiting.

Maybe he's not a superstar on Wall Street. Maybe he struggles to make it from paycheck to paycheck. Does that mean he is any less than those who have "made it"? I wish he would ease up on himself because, as far as human beings go, he is one of the best. He is a true friend. An independent thinker. A good son. A charitable person. A giver.

And yet, he feels inadequate. To me, the only thing that is inadequate is his paycheck. I wish some company would realize what a gem he is and reward him with a fabulous opportunity, but until that happens, he needs to lighten up on himself and realize what he *has* achieved in his time here. Seriously, how many people go through life thoroughly and unconditionally loved and adored by their families? How many people get the truest friends because *they* are the truest friends? How many people live lives of righteous goodness, where they naturally help and comfort others?

He's one of a kind, and that makes him a winner. I just wish he would see it and rewrite the story he is telling himself so he can be happy.

His story is perfect for a rewrite. Here's how I would handle it if that were my story script:

> *"I am changing my attitude because I realize I haven't fully appreciated my contribution in life. But, I am so grateful because I have the best family members – and I am loved by them. I have a safe home, I have good, true friends who appreciate and love*

me, and I have my relationship with God, which means everything to me. I have the brainpower to do big things and I am continuing in my job search with full confidence because I know things will work out. My self-esteem is strong because I am successful in every area that truly matters in life. I live well and love large. I am a good person. I have strong faith."

And, here are the affirmations I would add to the end:

I have a positive attitude about what I have accomplished in my life. I have won in every human category that counts.

I am happy every single day because I am blessed with such great people who love me so much.

I am energized in my job search because the right job will come my way as long as I keep trying.

Whenever I feel overwhelmed, I let go and let God help me.

I love myself. And, I like myself. I'm a great person who is smart, creative and fun to be around.

Other people see the good in me.

I see the good in myself and I celebrate it. All of my thoughts are positive. I believe wholeheartedly in myself.

He and I have talked about this so many times. Why won't he lighten up on himself? He's so hung up on his age because, the older he gets, the more he feels like he has failed. But he hasn't! He just won't open his eyes to his real success.

I finally asked him what he'd expect to be said when he is eulogized at his funeral. Will anyone there care what he did for a living? Will people be crying because of what he hasn't accomplished professionally? No! People will be devastated because of the loss of such a kind and true human being, a one-of-a-kind friend who made our lives rich with laughter, friendship and joy. People will grieve the loss of a bright light that spread so much happiness.

That is the true mark of a winner.

What are the greatest disappointments about what you have or haven't done with your life?

How often do you feel regret about these disappointments? Why?

How does that regret affect your self-esteem and self-confidence?

Can you still do some of the things you wish you'd done? What's stopping you?

Are you going to let go of your regrets or are you going to let them continue to make you have negative feelings?

When you are at the end of your life, will these disappointments make any difference?

Realizing What You Already Have

My old friend Billie just moved into her mother's home so she can keep her own house in pristine condition while she tries to sell it. The home is worth a fortune, and it must sell because she is a single parent who was laid off — another victim of the demise of daily newspapers.

I've known her for more than two decades, and I reminded her of the filthy apartment I helped her clean at the beach before she moved in. We were both in our 20s. She was my editor, mentor and friend. We made no money. But, *we lived at the beach.* We didn't go to fancy restaurants or take expensive trips. But, *we lived at the beach.* We drove old cars and didn't have any expendable income. But, *we lived at the beach.*

At the time, I was making $15,000 a year. I remember going out for payday dinner to Quincy's steak house and ordering the Kiddie Burger because it was the cheapest thing on the menu that came with the salad bar. I remember countless camping trips to the barrier islands in North Florida and South Georgia. I remember walking over a beach dune on Cumberland Island one night as the wild horses ran through the water, silhouetted by the heat lightning. And boating on the Okefenokee Swamp, surrounded by a million alligators. And tubing on the Ichetucknee River. Plus so many nights of youthful revelry with our cohorts.

Those were truly happy and fun times. I had so little money and so few things, but I had so much fun. I know I laughed more during those years than in any since. We were so young and carefree.

So, here we are. Years later, with nice houses and nice things, eating in fancy restaurants and enjoying the "best" of life. Looking at it now, I realize that we had the best of life when we didn't have very much at all.

Granted, Billie's situation is challenging because she is so devoted to her daughter and wants the best for her. It's so unfair — she's truly brilliant. But, she'll get through this.

She just will. And, if she scales back, maybe she'll remember how much fun it was when we didn't have so many "things" to worry about.

Last night, she reminded me how I once "punked" her when I sent her a letter that I'd forged on our publisher's letterhead. The letter told her that he'd heard she was complaining about her low salary and, while he couldn't give her any more money, he did want her to have a small token of his appreciation. Inside the envelope was a round button that had been wrapped in paper. Billie felt that package, figured it was a make-up compact, and what she assumed was the publisher's sexist gesture infuriated her. But when she unwrapped it, she discovered a button that said, "POVERTY SUCKS."

She found the letter recently — and the button. About "POVERTY SUCKS," she wrote: "I'm beginning to get the msg. 😃"

Maybe the message is that the poverty of our early years didn't suck all that much. When did we get so grown up that we forgot how rich we already were? I don't think I have ever been as rich as I was, way back when I was poor.

EXERCISE: Going Back to the Beginning

What did you expect out of life when you were 20 years old?

What did you think you would accomplish in your career?

What did you expect for your personal life?

How much money were you making?

What kind of housing did you have?

Were those the good old days? Why or why not?

Did you have simpler tastes when you were younger?

Plenty of people look back to their younger days as a time when they were footloose and fancy free. Were they?

Are there any ways to reconnect to that time when you had less but appreciated what you had more?

Would the person you were like the person you have become? What have you learned from that person? What would that person learn from what you have been through?

PERSPECTIVE

"Just think how happy you would be if you lost everything you have right now, and then got it back again "
– Author Frances Rodman

"Let us rise up and be thankful, for if we didn't learn a lot today, at least we learned a little, and if we didn't learn a little, at least we didn't get sick, and if we got sick, at least we didn't die; so, let us all be thankful."
– Buddha

"Gratefulness is the key to a happy life that we hold in our hands, because if we are not grateful, then no matter how much we have we will not be happy -- because we will always want to have something else or something more."
– David Steindl-Rast, Theologian

"You say grace before meals. All right. But I say grace before the concert and the opera, and grace before the play and pantomime, and grace before I open a book, and grace before sketching, painting, swimming, fencing, boxing, walking, playing, dancing and grace before I dip the pen in the ink."
– G. K. Chesterton, English Writer

"If the only prayer you said in your whole life was, "thank you," that would suffice."
– Meister Eckhart, German Theologian and Philosopher

"Gratitude unlocks the fullness of life. It turns what we have into enough, and more. It turns denial into acceptance, chaos into order, confusion into clarity.... It turns problems into gifts, failures into success, the unexpected into perfect timing, and mistakes into important events. Gratitude makes sense of our past, brings peace for today and creates a vision for tomorrow." – Melodie Beattie, Author

"What you focus on expands, and when you focus on the goodness in your life, you create more of it. Opportunities, relationships, even money flowed my way when I learned to be grateful no matter what happened in my life."
-- Oprah Winfrey

"There is no such thing as gratitude unexpressed. If it is unexpressed, it is plain, old-fashioned ingratitude."
– Robert Brault, Writer and Poet

Okay, there is a lot of medicine in those quotes on gratitude because they center us and remind us that we already have so much in life.

The first quote – from Frances Rodman – is a quick awakening to the fact that we have so much that we value. But do you see it? Do you feel gratitude for what you have or do you take it for granted?

Exercise: Take a minute to re-read the quotes here. Think about them, center yourself, then write an essay about the gratitude you feel for what you already have. Refer back to this essay whenever you are feeling low, because gratitude has the magic ability to bring sad people back around to the light.

Confused About Your Purpose in Life? It's Simple.

Several years ago, I quit my job to chase my dream of writing a book, but that book was rejected repeatedly. I was demoralized. If I wasn't going to be "Fawn Germer, Author," who would I be? Everybody was asking, "How's the book coming?" "When's the book coming out?" I felt like such a failure. I was so embarrassed.

My friends got together one day and I blurted out, *"I don't know my purpose in life."* The outburst was met with silence and stares. Finally, my friend Pam said, "I don't know, either." She was in a job she hated. Teresa said, "Me either." One by one, we went around the room and every single one of us confessed that we didn't know our purpose in life.

I was sure that, by the time we got to Bette, we would get an answer. Bette was in the throes of chemotherapy for ovarian cancer and, surely she had figured things out since she was facing a likely terminal outcome. But she shook her head "no."

Not one of us knew our purpose in life.

Time passed. I sold my book. Pam switched jobs, Teresa went back to school and Bette kept on living as best she could.

For two years, Bette lived the best life possible. Once, we went kayaking to Caladesi Island. The Gulf of Mexico was cold, yet she dove right in because she said she thought "the water was pretty." She got a grant from the city to build a butterfly garden in her neighborhood. She spent time with family and went hiking and laughed and lived.

My book was finally published and Bette and the gang made it to my first big signing. It was a big deal for her, and she'd forced herself to rally so she could be there to support me. A day or two later, she was in the hospital again. I left on tour for several weeks, and when I got back, she began her walk into death. One day, she told me she'd seen Jesus and she wasn't afraid.

The day came when her brother called to let me know Bette had passed away. He asked if I would write her obituary. As a journalist, I have always thought that obituaries are the most important things we will ever write because they are the last word on an individual's life. I spent a lot of time writing Bette's. I thought about how she'd lived her life as she faced her death. She filled every moment with as much joy as she could find. She was from a huge family and every one of her brothers and sisters took turns coming down for a week and caring for her. I know that, when she died, there was peace. She'd defined her purpose in life by simply living her life. That obituary was not a list of accomplishments. It was the story of a woman who *lived.* Regardless of what life threw at her, she lived.

That was when I realized what I'd learned through her passing. Our purpose in life is to live our lives. In the end, the only thing that matters is that we breathed in our moment here and filled it with life.

I was flying off to St. Louis for an event the next morning and everything was so rushed because I'd taken time to write the obituary. I had to get my hair cut before my trip and was going to a new hair salon. I passed right by it as I sped through the darkness, then turned around on the busy six-lane road and kept searching for the salon. I moved into the two-way turn lane so I could see the numbers better on the left side of the street, but that was a terrible, terrible miscalculation. Another car was coming straight toward me, blaring his horn. We had no time to stop and nowhere to go because there was so much traffic whizzing past in the other lanes.

Miraculously, a space opened up on his side and he moved into it, flipping me off as he sped past me.

Seconds later, I turned into the salon parking lot. My heart was pounding harder than it ever had. I'd come within a split second of being killed. How tragic it was, because my friend had just died after spending two years fighting so hard to live, and I had almost died because I hadn't been paying attention.

What a profound lesson. We lose so much time by not paying attention and don't realize what we are wasting until we face losing it. It doesn't matter what you do for your job or where you are living or where you think you rank in society. What matters is what you do today to live and enjoy your life.

It's so simple. Your purpose in life is to live your life.

What is *your* "purpose in life"?

Do you keep things in perspective or do you need to make changes?

What can you tell yourself to keep you focused on what truly matters?

Letting Go of Your Need for Control

"If everything seems under control, you're just not going fast enough."
Racer Mario Andretti

I always say, "Make a plan for what you want to do with your life. It's the greatest piece of fiction you will ever write."

Truly. Life unfolds. You cannot force, command, direct, ordain, bully, manage or control it. You just can't. As soon as you think you have everything all figured out, you slam right into an obstacle. There goes your plan.

If we could control life, we'd all have millions in the bank, excellent health, gorgeous spouses or partners, perfectly behaved children, fully functional families and, well, you get what I mean. Life would be oh-so-pretty on any given day. It would be predictable and it would be fair.

It would also be boring.

There is so much in life that is out of our control, yet we feel some urge to manage the unmanageable, to achieve the outcome *we* want. We want people to think, react and behave the way we want them to. We want our efforts to be successful. We want to know where we are headed, but sometimes we just can't.

You could be on the greatest run of your career, only to find out that you have cancer. You get it together, adjust your plan for what is ahead and gear up to do what you have to do to beat the disease. But sometimes it isn't up to you. Sometimes, life comes at you in ways that are brutal and unfair. It's all part of the growth experience.

You can't control what happens to you, but you *can* control your reaction. Look at how many people have been shocked to learn their spouses have been cheating or living secret lives. And how many people have devoted their lives to companies that were quick to dismiss them when times got tough. Look how many people thought they had secure retirements, only to see their investments disappear.

Life is fragile and unpredictable. It turns on a dime. One day you are healthy, the next day you are not. One day you are happily married, the next day you are not. One day you are gainfully employed, the next day you are not. We are constantly faced with an uncertainty that is so unsettling to some that, rather than learning to ride the waves, they try in vain to control the tide.

Life can't be controlled.

You Don't Want Your Life Micromanaged, So Why Are You Micromanaging Others?

There are star-crossed lovers who find each other because "opposites attract," only to later try to change each other because what attracted them in the first place is now annoying the hell out of them. They needle and criticize and argue because they now can't tolerate their differences, wishing only for some modicum of control over the other's behavior.

There are parents who try to micromanage their children's lives in order to fast-track them to success. They get them in the right classes in the right schools with the right nudges that will lead them to the right path. The only problem is, they are grooming their children to live out their parents' dreams and expectations, rather than their own.

There are bosses who try to micromanage everything in order to control the outcome, and what do they accomplish? They alienate their people, get no buy-in or support, and ultimately scramble to achieve their goals.

And there are people who push their control issues to extremes, bullying others to the point that they are afraid to come and go or make friends or eat certain foods or pray a certain way.

From the outside looking in, it sure seems like people try to control others so they feel in control of themselves. If only you can get everything to fall into place the way *you* think they should fall into place, then you'll find peace of mind, right?

How does it feel when someone is trying to control you? Not good. I kind of like my free will, and I'm pretty sure you like it, too. I don't like someone telling me when or where or how or why. I like to feel that others respect and value my judgment enough to let me do my best – whether the issue is professional or personal. I have come to accept and love my eccentricities because, after all, those are the traits that define me as an individual – even if they may be quirky or nonconforming. That said, I welcome constructive criticism because others can see places where I can improve my game. But I don't welcome the hovering presence of a control freak who is so neurotic that he or she can't let me be my best self.

You probably feel that way, too. And while you are sensitive to the infringements that come when others try to control you, are you sensitive to what you might be doing to violate the control boundaries of others? Do you tell others what to do? How to do it? When? Do your suggestions seem more like orders? Do they feel compelled to act on what you say, or at least respond to it? Truthfully, are you trying to run anyone else's life or control their performance? If so, why?

How have you tried to control how other people perform, behave or produce?

Did they think you may have been a little heavy-handed?

Did you get the results you wanted?

What would have happened if you'd been a little more hands off?

Did your interference make your people perform better in the short term, but build resentment that will affect results in the long term?

Okay, now the flip side. Take a minute to think of a situation where you felt you were being over-controlled and manipulated.

Describe the situation where you were the victim of a controlling person's influence.

How did it make you feel?

Did you perform better than if you'd done it your way?

How did it affect your attitude?

Have you often felt that others have put too much energy into controlling what you do? How has that affected your attitude? Performance? Self-esteem?

Have you expressed concerns in these situations? What have you said?

How were your concerns received?

Did anything change? What? Do you need to make additional changes?

You Choose Your Micromanagers

I am inclined to fight back when someone tries to micromanage me. But I am floored by the legions of people who find themselves in jobs, relationships, friendships and other situations where they get pushed around. There is certainly no shortage of controlling partners who will pick away until they have wiped out the confidence and self-direction of their less-assertive partner. If you find yourself being pushed around by someone who acts like he or she knows better than you – whether it is at home or at work – you have to take responsibility for giving your power away. You are the one allowing it and you've got to ask yourself why. Do you need someone to tell you how to do things *their* way or do you need to find someone who respects you enough to let you do it yourself? If the situation is at work and it is making you miserable, why are you staying?

In extreme cases, a controlling relationship is often labeled "emotionally abusive." That's a term that makes women (and men) stop in their tracks to think what is going on, why they are taking it and what they need to do. But there are legions of men and women who have emotionally abusive relationships at work. Because the abusers are generally bosses or managers who affect paychecks, promotions and careers, their victims are more reluctant to set boundaries that honor their dignity and let them do their best work. If you are in an emotionally abusive relationship at work, you have to decide how helpless you really are.

Whether the emotional abuser is at work or at home, there comes a point when you have to make choices – at the risk of the relationship – in order to salvage your individual self. You have to honor who you are, or you are no one at all.

If your boyfriend or husband won't let you have any time to yourself, there comes a point when you have to make the choice to protect your sanity. It is up to you to set your own boundaries.

At work, it can be trickier. When the risk is great and the stakes are high (like when the economy tanks and it is hard to find other jobs), it may be time to hold back and wait. But ultimately, you are in charge of your own sanity. You can set boundaries for bullies and control freaks, but you have to size them up first.

I have had more than one bullying boss, and I learned to deal with them in different ways. One guy was a usually loveable teddy bear of a man, but he had a terrible temper that would blow before he got all the information he needed. This was back when I was a reporter and he blew up at me in the middle of the newsroom, yelling at me in front of about 30 people because he thought I didn't do an assignment. Problem was, I'd done it – *he* had just looked for it in the wrong computer file. I had to set a boundary.

"Don't ever yell at me in public like that again," I told him as I pulled him into his office. "It is unprofessional and I am not going to take it. Second, I did the assignment. It's right where it is supposed to be. You have made a big scene out there based on your bad information and now you need to go out there and publicly set the record straight." And he did. He apologized right in front of everyone.

But, another bullying boss would blow up at everybody and, when he blew up at me, there was no setting him straight. That was the way he was. He didn't care about being fair or decent. He didn't care about how we felt about how we were treated. He walked around the room with his "I'm the boss!" attitude and, believe me, he *was* the boss. At least, until I decided that he wasn't. I got another job and **I** fired **him**. How empowering!

It is amazing how much power an individual can have over you until you decide you have had enough and take the steps to make a change. In this case, I had enough, updated my resume and got another job. Once I moved on, he couldn't control another single thing in my life.

There are always so many variables that influence the what, when, why and how of a situation, and it is important that you focus on them. This is a workbook, so I don't want to oversimplify the enormity of these situations or even minimize them by saying some of these relationship issues are on the same level as work relationship issues. I've written other books that look at these issues, but this is the book where *you* need to look at them and see if there are connections between control issues at work and at home. Finally, you have to ask yourself some questions:

Do I attract people in my life who feel it is okay to control me or push me around? What might I be doing that makes it seem okay to do that to me?

Is this a rare issue for me or have I had problems with it historically – at work and at home? Is it always the other person's fault?

What might I have done differently in the past to put the controllers in their place? What can I learn from those situations?

When others have control over you, it is because you have relinquished your power to them. You are not a prison inmate who has given up your right to live and breathe in the way that you choose, but the decision about whether to stay in controlling relationships and controlling work environments is yours alone.

You can fire your boss. You can dump a bullying spouse or partner. It may not seem like you are in charge of your own life, but you are.

I am the boss of me. If I had my way, everything would go my way. I'd be fabulously rich, my relationships would be perfectly sweet, I would never experience frustration or disappointment or rejection or embarrassment or…

But that is a delusional fantasy. We do not live in a world where everything goes our way. So why is it that so many people waste so much energy trying to force the universe into submission? Life is pretty much an out-of-control experience. All we can control is our ability to rock and roll with it and enjoy the ride.

Life is Simply an Out-of-Control Experience

I know someone who has micro-scheduled six days of her week into 10-minute increments and gives herself a break on the seventh day, when it's only in 30-minute blocks. I have one friend who has literally written a business plan for her online dating experience. And another friend who uses Excel spreadsheets to plan every potentiality in life, whether it is concerning a vacation or her workout regime.

Do you try to control too much? A lot of people do this because they are so worried about achieving perfection that they try to manipulate every element of a situation. Once you let go of that need for perfection, you can let go of a need to control.

Just be, just do.

Let go. There is a calming peace that washes over you when you make the decision to be *excellent* – rather than perfect. You get a lot more accomplished. You are a better decision-maker when you don't have to plan for every possibility. Sometimes, you don't need an A+ in every subject. Heaven help you – you can make peace with an A- or, God forbid, a B. Chill out, already.

Look at the things you are trying to influence or control. Be honest about yourself.

Are you bossing others around in a way that diminishes their ability to do their best? Why?

Are you minding *your* turf or your turf plus other peoples' turf? Why?

Are you assuming responsibility, control or credit for things that others rightly think belong to them? Why?

Do you feel like you have to solve every predicament? Why?

Are you the only one who can fix these situations? Why?

How do you think others will view you if you don't handle all of these problems? Why?

Do you tend to think your people are not as capable or responsible as you? Why?

Does that make you interfere with their lives? Why?

Do you feel like things would work much better if everyone followed your directions? Why?

Do other people need you to show them what to do and keep them on track? Why?

Do you think you will be judged harshly if your people don't deliver stellar results? Why?

What is the worst thing that will happen if you let others find their own way and do their own thing? Why?

Do you feel you won't be seen as "needed" if you aren't directing others on what to do and how to do it? Why?

The same goes at home. You all know parents who micromanage their children in an effort to guide them toward great success. They push too hard. They think of all kinds of activities that their children "should" do, and soon the poor kid is playing a musical instrument he cares nothing about while studying accounting at night and playing soccer, even though he doesn't like music, math or sports. While a certain amount of guidance is necessary, your kids have to live their own lives. At some point you have to realize that your job is not to blaze their trail, but rather to help them find their own way. I have one very well-meaning friend who enrolled her children in private school and did their homework for them because she thought the teachers were expecting too much. That is not right – any more than it is right for a manager to do an employee's assignment because the employee can't do it as well.

And, let me confess right here – I made that mistake as a manager when I was a newspaper editor. I had a strong background as an investigative reporter and one of the writers I inherited was only good at light features. She was incredibly slow. At first, I would sit next to her and teach her what she needed to know in order to do the story. She just couldn't get it. She would come in to write on a deadline, then deliver an absolute mess several hours later. I would end up going home at 10 or 11 at night instead of at 6:30 p.m. It ticked me off.

She did not get any better and my boss didn't want to hear about her performance. Eventually, it got to the point that the reporter would come in with her notes, then sit next to me as I'd write her story for her. The story would be just right and I'd get out at 6:30 or 7. But what a terrible thing to do to an employee. I should have helped her as much as possible, and if she continued to fail at her job, I should have made the case to have her reassigned or demoted.

Cut it out. If people can't perform up to your *reasonable* expectations, get people who will. Otherwise, let your people do their thing.

Controlling Your Control Issues

1. Let go and realize you can't control or solve everything.

2. Take a hard look at what you are doing. Are you worrying about your performance or everybody else's?

3. Decide whether you are making choices that put you in the victim role and make the decision to change your pattern.

4. Set boundaries when you feel you are being controlled. If the controller doesn't respect them, decide how to minimize the person's impact on your life.

5. Ask others if they feel you are being too controlling or manipulative. Ask how this is affecting them and what you can do better.

6. Let go of the need for perfection. Once you decide that "Excellence is good enough," you don't have to micromanage every little thing in hopes of achieving perfection. The truth is, there is no perfection.

Let Go, Let God

There are plenty of situations that you can't fix. You just can't. They will play out one way or another, but you can't control, fix or change things to guarantee your end result. You can try to achieve control, but if you are being honest, you are completely powerless.

You've heard the saying, "Let go and let God." I will bring up spirituality every now and again, but I am careful not to tell anyone what to believe. I just hope you believe in something, because life sure does seem to work better when you do – especially when it comes to trying to control things that can't be controlled. A friend forwarded me the following memo in an e-mail and I printed it out and keep it posted on my computer:

MEMO FROM GOD:

To: YOU
Date: TODAY
From: GOD
Subject: YOURSELF
Reference: LIFE

This is God. Today I will be handling All of your problems for you. I do NOT need your help. So, have a nice day. I love you.

Love,
God

P.S. And, remember... If life happens to deliver a situation to you that you cannot handle, do not attempt to resolve it yourself! Kindly put it in the SFGTD (something for God to do) box. I will get to it in MY TIME. All situations will be resolved, but in My time, not yours.

Once the matter is placed into the box, do not hold onto it by worrying about it. Instead, focus on all the wonderful things that are present in your life now.

Sometimes we need to step out of the chaos that consumes our days and remember that most of our worries are really not such big deals. Sometimes, we can pass the buck on worrying by handing problems or issues over to the universe.

There truly are times when we are powerless. There is power in recognizing that and letting go in order to let a higher power step in. If we can't control or fix something, why do we spend so much time trying? Let it go.

I think God likes helping me out. I used to be careful not to ask for help in matters that I thought I could control for myself, but then I started reading books that told me that God will help when asked. So, I started asking. I found a new calm when I realized I didn't have to carry the weight of every challenge by myself. I know I bear some responsibility for my life, but I don't feel like I have to handle anything by myself. With my spiritual connection, I have a partnership that makes every experience bigger, fuller and richer. I'm not doing anything alone, and that is a meaningful definition of life for me. Again, I'm not telling you what to believe. I just hope you believe something because I believe life makes more sense when it's lived in partnership with God.

I once moderated a panel with senior executives and asked them how spirituality had impacted their careers. All of them said it was the most important influence they had. But one of the successful women in corporate America stopped the show when she looked at that audience and said, "I can guarantee that at least 95 percent of the people in this audience are smarter than I am. I would have done nothing *without* God's help." It was such a memorable moment.

Why do we obsess about controlling that which can't be controlled, or solving that which can't be solved? Maybe it's ego. Maybe we fear that we don't "have what it takes" instead of accepting that no one does. Much of life is unsolvable. You can face that reality and feel either impotence or relief. You don't have to be so smart and strong and savvy and connected and powerful that you can drive the elements to a win every time. No one can do that. You can't guarantee the sun will shine tomorrow, that others will behave as you or others expect and deserve, that the economy will rebound, that you will win a contest or plenty of other things. But, if you let go of that need to control, it is amazing how much better you will do.

Set Goals That You Can "Control"

As a reporter, I could not control whether I won a Pulitzer Prize. I couldn't control the competition or the judging. I couldn't control the politics or the reputation of the newspaper that selected nominees. I couldn't control plenty of things, so I definitely couldn't control whether I won or not. Why have that as a goal? I didn't.

Early in my career, reporter Randy Loftis told me to set goals that I *could* control. "You can't control whether you win a Pulitzer," he said, "but you can control whether you do Pulitzer-quality work."

You can't control whether you get a promotion, but you can control whether you do the quality of work that is needed in order to get that promotion. You can't control whether you get a certain person to fall in love with you, but you can control the things you do to make yourself attractive to a certain kind of person. So take a minute to reconfigure your goals. See if you have structured them so that they are within your control. If not, rewrite them so you can control their outcomes. I'll show you a few of mine as examples:

Goal I can't control	Goal I can control
I want to write a book that sells a million copies.	I will write a great book that I market and position so it has the potential of selling a million copies.
I want to win the lottery.	I'll buy a ticket so I have a chance of winning the lottery.
I want to get my book on Oprah.	I will send press releases and copies of my book to Oprah's producers and stick with it so I know they have seen my book and made a decision.
I want to double my speaking business this year.	I will do a new business plan, put together a new press kit, brainstorm with my mastermind group, then magnify my marketing efforts in order to position myself to double my speaking business this year.

Okay, now you do it with your most important goals.

Goal I can't control	Goal I can control

Affirmations to Begin Your Change Process

I accept that I cannot control every situation.

I easily let go of things I cannot control.

I feel my strength when others try to control me, and I set appropriate boundaries.

I have let go of the need for perfection.

When I become overwhelmed, I let go and give my problems to the universe.

Life is an out-of-control experience. I enjoy the ride every single day because I am learning and growing.

I am in control of my own self and make my own decisions.

Deciding to Decide

My cousin Howard met the love of his life on the Internet. He lived in Michigan, she lived in Minnesota. Soon after they started corresponding, he flew out for a visit. Two days later, he asked her to marry him.

Sophia laughs about it because, ten years later, she knows how Howard makes decisions. It is never done on a whim. "He'll be looking at socks and it'll be, 'Do I want blue ones or brown ones? Or blue ones with dots on them or brown ones with stripes?' And he'll spend forever trying to decide on those socks."

But he knew so quickly that she was the one for him, right when he met her.

And so it goes with decision making.

Sometimes you know, sometimes you don't.

The challenge is letting go when you aren't certain, because life moves way too fast for endless hesitation. These days, you've got to decide to decide.

The days of 100 percent certainty and perfect timing are long gone. Things change so quickly now that you have to be secure enough to take a chance. You just have to know that you are smart enough to make good decisions and savvy enough to recover and learn from the ones that are not so good.

But how can you learn to give up on certainty if you are one who naturally likes to deliberate until you feel confident and comfortable that your ducks are all lined up and you are guaranteed a successful result?

Your Role as a Decision Maker

Before working on the decisions, work on your role as the decision-maker. Work on your own confidence so you become more naturally adept at action plans and recovery. Things used to move slower because there was no alternative. We can now send massive documents to the other side of the world by pushing a button, or convene a meeting via conference call or videoconference that makes it possible for people from different cities, states or continents to be in the same place at the same time.

Rating Yourself as a Decision-Maker	Always	Usually	Sometimes	Rarely	Never
I like making decisions.					
I am known as a good decision-maker.					
I like to delay decisions as long as possible.					
I make the right decisions.					
I work out decisions with lists or charts that help clarify my thinking.					
Once I make a decision, I let go of it and stop worrying whether I made a mistake.					
I take full responsibility for my decisions.					
I stay on track to make a decision as quickly as I reasonably can.					

Rating Yourself as a Decision-Maker	Always	Usually	Sometimes	Rarely	Never
I am calm and relaxed when faced with a tough decision.					
I let go of the endless "what ifs" when I am making a decision.					
I quickly determine when a decision is not working and recalibrate to get a better outcome.					
A fear of failing doesn't hold me back from my decision-making.					
When I make a mistake, I learn from it and move on.					
I make decisions, rather than letting things happen by default.					

Award 4 points for every "ALWAYS"

Award 3 points for every "USUALLY"

Award 2 points for every "SOMETIMES"

Award 1 point for every "RARELY"

Award 0 points for every "NEVER"

49 to 56 points: You know when you have to make a decision and you make it. You do your research, come to a conclusion and decide, but you don't let things end there. You monitor the situation to see if you need to modify your course. You don't kill yourself if you make a mistake. If you don't make a decision, it is because you have consciously decided not to do it, which is a decision in itself.

36 to 48 points: You're a good decision-maker. In fact, you will often charge ahead, get your information straight, weigh the possibilities and come up with the best answer. It may stress you out, but you do what you have to do.

23 to 35 points: You aren't great at making decisions and will sometimes put things off until they take their own course. But you can sit down and deliberate and come to a conclusion when you have to. That doesn't mean you enjoy it.

14 to 22 points: You don't like decisions, you don't have confidence when it is time to make them and you second-guess yourself plenty. You'll readily admit you need to work on this.

Fewer than 14 points: You are a terrible decision-maker. You worry things to death or do nothing. You hound yourself about mistakes and are paralyzed when it comes to deciding.

I don't have to tell you how fast things move. In my lifetime, we went from relying on newspapers and the six o'clock news to being able to view news live – through a cell phone. This is an instantaneous world. There is no room for slow-pokes.

My parents' generation was taught to write out "pro" and "con" lists to consider the good and bad of decisions. The problem with that approach is, decisions aren't completely black or white, and they aren't all good or bad. More than that, not all considerations are equal when weighing a decision.

For example, you may be a guy considering marriage to a woman. Should the fact that she is an excellent cook be weighted equally with the fact that she's a serious alcoholic? No! Some things trump others. Or you are house hunting. Should the fact that it has a nice pool outweigh the fact that it is built on top of a sinkhole? Granted, the pros and cons are drastic in these examples, but you get the idea. When the answers are less obvious, figure out the trump issues.

We are constantly making decisions that impact our lives and the lives of others. The consequences can be huge – and lasting. A simple pro-con list doesn't account for the fact that, sometimes, one important "pro" outweighs fifty less important "cons." So, how do we let go of our fears and make hard decisions?

For one thing, it takes a conscious decision to be a decision-maker. You are going to make a lot of decisions in this life. Some will be great, some won't. Hopefully, you'll be right more than you will be wrong, but it is inevitable that you will make some mistakes – and some will be real doozies. Big deal. A bad decision just presents you with another opportunity to be a strategic problem-solver. It also teaches you something you can use in the future.

Nobody is perfect. The person who has a perfect track record making decisions is someone who likely hasn't made a lot of decisions, or someone who has not flung himself or herself into the kinds of decisions that are most challenging and risky.

It is easy to put off one decision, then find out that it has led you to the point where you have to make an even bigger decision or, perhaps, several additional decisions. Why not just deal with things as they come?

The other thing is, many, many decisions seem so vital at the time, but really aren't that big of a deal once time passes and you look back on things. Try to take a "big picture" look at the situation and ask yourself if it will be of concern to you in a year or two or five.

What's the Problem?

There is a saying that "We are too busy mopping the floor to turn off the faucet." Aren't we a brilliant species? So many of us start cleaning up our messes without ever figuring out what caused it in the first place. And we can mop and mop and mop and mop, but that floor will never be clean because the problem is not the floor, it is the faucet.

See? Brilliant.

Know what the problem is before you decide how to fix it. Then, FIX IT.

Years ago, I moved to a relatively new home and soon realized that the light in the garage was quite a fickle fixture. If I turned the switch on, the light wouldn't come on. If I flicked the switch on and off a couple of times, it would. After a couple of years, it got even more fickle. I'd flick it on and off very carefully, sometimes only going halfway in hopes that it would signal the fluorescent tubes to come on. On and off, on and off, on and off until, finally, it came on.

After six years of that – I repeat, SIX YEARS, I happened to be in Home Depot and notice some fluorescent tubes that seemed to be exactly the right size. Could that have been the problem, and not the light switch? I bought two tubes and thought I would give it a shot.

I brought the tubes home, got out the ladder, took out the old tubes and installed the new ones.

Then came the moment when I went over to the light switch, and flipped it on. To my amazement, the lights came right on. That very first time. It took me five minutes and two $1.99 fluorescent tubes to cure six years of annoyance.

Wouldn't it have made sense to just focus on the problem, come up with a solution and get on with things? Of course! But, no. I just found a way around the problem – hitting that light switch repeatedly like a lab rat for six years – rather than taking a few minutes to analyze it and come up with a solution.

We do that.

We avoid problem analysis and dance around trying to come up with easy fixes that don't really address the issue. We triage our difficulties to the point that easy things are never addressed, and over time, become extended annoyances or worse. We anguish over decisions, fearing that we might do the wrong thing, instead of embracing them as opportunities to define ourselves, our world and our future. We choose to keep mopping that floor without ever finding out why it is wet in the first place.

Look at your problems. Acknowledge them. Define them. Define the possibilities. Strategize solutions. Then, start making decisions.

Sounds so easy, but sometimes we find ourselves in stressful situations where we feel paralyzed, and we use denial to keep us from really addressing the problem and taking care of it. If you are drowning in debt, letting your bills pile up unopened doesn't help you fix the problem. It makes things worse. If you find a lump in your breast, waiting for it to go away is a pretty dumb strategy.

You can't be a competent problem solver or decision-maker without being willing to face the situations that are causing you stress. Obstacles are inevitable in this life, but they will not destroy you unless you give them permission to destroy you.

"The problem is not that there are problems. The problem is expecting otherwise and thinking that having problems is a problem," wrote psychiatrist and author Theodore Isaac Rubin.

So right, Dr. Rubin. So right.

Once we accept that we are going to have challenges, it is just a matter of coming up with a system that helps us deal with them.

One reminder: Focus on your decisions. Delegate what you should delegate. Sometimes we get so wrapped up in the issues that we don't step back and consider whether someone else should be doing the decision-making. Don't pass the buck when you are sitting right where it is supposed to stop. And don't grab someone else's buck and rob them of the power to make their own decisions.

Besides, you have enough to worry about. There are times in your life when our list of woes could go on for pages. Looking at a list of 100 problems that need addressing is a sure-fire way to cause you to give up before you even try. Obviously, we've got to prioritize. Categorize. Decide what is immediate, what is critical, and what you can put on hold. Don't confuse "immediate" with "critical." Immediate means you've got to deal with things now, but these concerns aren't necessarily the most important issues on your list. Those "critical" problems that you might get away with delaying in the background for some time can ultimately mushroom into the worst kinds of concerns -- ones that are both critical *and* immediate.

Rating What's On Your Plate	SOMEWHAT IMPORTANT	IMPORTANT	CRITICAL	IMMEDIATE	SHORT TERM	LONG TERM

Directions: Use the above table to rate the issues you are concerned with at this time. Those that are both "critical" and "immediate" should be done first. "Somewhat important" and "long term" can wait. You get the idea.

When you look at your list of problems in the above list, rank them and decide what needs addressing first. Make sure you review the ones you've decided to let simmer for a while, and calculate the cost of neglecting them.

Just write a list and look at it. More than anything, know what is waiting to be dealt with, and start dealing with things. Life doesn't get out of control all by itself. Sometimes we help it by deliberately ignoring the things that should not be ignored. So, if you have to make one of these painful lists of all the challenges on your plate, go ahead and do it. It sure beats what happens when you close your eyes, hope for the best and find out that hope does very little to solve the problems that demand your time and attention.

The good thing about making a list of all the issues you have to deal with is this: Sometimes you take a good look at a problem and realize it is not such a big deal. And you can also review your assessment with others who might add more perspective and a fresher viewpoint to help you come up with a plan.

So, the basic questions:

- WHO should make the decision?

- WHAT is the problem? WHAT are the signs that something is wrong?

- WHO does it affect? WHO or WHAT seems to be making matters worse? See and acknowledge your own role in the situation. Don't automatically jump into blame mode here. Just define who is involved.

- WHERE is it occurring?

- WHEN is it happening?

- HOW has it evolved?

- WHY is it going on?

Once you've done that cursory review, you are in a position to write a summary that outlines what is wrong, what you want to happen, and why things are not working. This works well to outline basic issues that confront us daily.

The simple summary system is not the best way to attack complicated problems because it lacks the depth you will need to analyze a significant issue. But if you break down a major issue into its parts, then do the cursory review and summary steps for each of those parts, you will have defined something quite complicated in a way that will help you to work on a solution.

What are your options?

While evaluating your decision, begin by reviewing your intent and overall objectives. Intent is critical, because it shapes your vision of what you are trying to achieve.

Really immerse yourself in the process of critical thinking. As long as you remain mindful of your mission and objectives, you can approach decision-making with clarity and conduct the process with purpose. Always remember your big picture objectives.

Then, start looking at your options. Brainstorm the possibilities, from the most realistic to the most far-fetched. Give yourself permission to be creative and wild and even stupid about it, because that frees you to think outside your limits. Write everything down. Combine, delete, expand and twist your ideas until you've come up with a list that gives you some *real* options to consider.

Fear leads us to make decisions on other peoples' timetables or constrains us from doing what we know is right in our gut. Sometimes it is important to do what is most popular, sometimes it is not. Just explore everything. Take a contrarian approach to this process, so that you can flip every possibility on its side and come up with even more options. Instead of launching a program in six weeks, do it in two. Or twelve. Instead of placing the obvious person in charge of the program, put the last one anyone would expect in charge. Instead of painting the wall white, go with red. Don't be afraid to consider the bizarre or seemingly impossible. Just brainstorm so you have a full menu of options. And then, if you want to go with something predictable, you have at least considered a wide range of possibilities.

Assess the risk

I am a great advocate for risk-taking, but I always tell people to assess and fortify their risks. After you have gone through that process, spend time in risk assessment mode. This is such a critical step in the decision-making process, but it is one that is too often overlooked. It is astonishing how some people will make an instant decision without taking the time to assess the consequences or fallout of their actions. Spend time seriously looking at the "what if" scenarios – not to scare yourself out of doing something risky, but to help you act from an informed position of strength, rather than ignorance or impulse.

Really assess what might go wrong. What is the worst case scenario? How likely is it that things will play out that way? What is the most likely outcome? How difficult will it be to mitigate damage from the fallout?

Asking those kinds of questions can only help you to clarify your vision and resolve. This process prepares you for action. It also gives you the information you need when and if you need to make adjustments. And, it keeps you from looking like an idiot.

1. What is the main issue you have to deal with? What's your timetable?

2. What are you worried about?

3. What do you have to gain?

4. What do you have to lose?

5. What is the most obvious solution?

6. What is the less obvious solution?

7. What's the worst thing that could happen?

8. What is the likelihood that the worst thing will happen?

Leave Your Bubble

A lifetime ago, I worked as a reporter for a company that was locked in one of the most bloody newspaper wars in the country. When I got there, our circulation soared above the competition and it looked like we'd won the war. But, in came a couple of dopey executives who blew our circulation lead and soon, the competition was on top and we were the underdogs. Our circulation continued to plunge. And plunge.

Every decision designed to resuscitate our circulation numbers came down to us from above in the form of a dictate. How we were going to write. When we were going to write. When we were going to run stories. They wanted more conservative editorials, less book coverage, more weather stories and, well, it just went on.

The thing was, they *never* asked us what we thought would improve readership numbers, yet we were the people out there on our beats and working in the community, constantly talking with readers. They never left their offices to ask the readers who were, after all, their customers. They just brainstormed in isolation, and figured they knew best what they would force down the public's throat.

Because my paper and its rival were committed to putting each other out of business, both undercut each other and both newspapers had the lowest advertising rates, subscription rates and newsstand rates in the United States.

One of the crazier decisions was to raise the newsstand cost of the paper from 25 cents to 35 cents. Now, I am not Einstein, but think about it. You have two news racks outside a restaurant, and one has a paper in it that costs a quarter, and the other has one that requires the customer to fish out a quarter *and* a dime. And, the two papers aren't that different and both have most of the same stories. What do you think happened? Right. Circulation took a speedy nosedive, losing tens of thousands of sales every day.

I was friendly with the publisher, and I remember the day he told me he was firing the circulation director who had cooked up that idea.

"He said we'd lose a small percentage of our circulation, but nothing like this," the publisher said.

"Where did he get his projections?" I asked.

"Well, I asked him that yesterday," he said. (Seriously? Why hadn't he asked the guy that *before* he raised the price?) "He admitted it had been a guess."

Oh. It had been a guess.

Who was the bigger fool? The guy who guessed, or the publisher who put our company's future on the line without asking the most basic question of the person who was informing him for the decision? Why hadn't the publisher asked, "Where did you get your information?" Why hadn't he demanded charts of the projections, or background on what had happened in other competitive markets when newsstand prices were increased? Would he have risked everything, had he known the future of the newspaper was being undermined by a mere guess?

The risk was huge. It was one of a handful of really stupid decisions that eventually led to the newspaper – the legendary *Rocky Mountain News* –shutting down in 2009. I could detail the other bad decisions, but they all illustrate the very same point. You don't make decisions without doing your homework on the fallout and consequences. You do try different things, but you fortify the risks you take so you have the greatest opportunity to succeed.

Would you buy a home without getting it inspected? Would you marry someone you knew nothing about? Would you move to a city without spending time there? Would you invest money with someone who promises fantastic returns without making sure to the person is not a con artist? Would you have major surgery without getting a second opinion?

Sure, people do those things all the time. Most get disastrous results. Get information. Do your homework. Inform yourself by leaving your bubble and critically analyzing what you are deciding.

More than anything, talk to people. Other people see things we overlook. Their experience and perspective can give you valuable insight. If you don't bring together a "kitchen cabinet" of friends and advisors who can help you make an informed decision, you should ask yourself why.

Why would you think you are so brilliant that you don't benefit from outside counsel when confronted by new and substantial problems? Don't other people have different perspectives and approaches that can help you come up with something innovative that might actually work? Are you afraid of outside input because you are too controlling? Are you too arrogant to believe others may have ideas worth considering?

As you turn off the autopilot and realign your strategies, be open to other ideas and approaches that will expand your possibilities and probabilities. Two heads are better than one. Five are better than two. You don't have to interview a thousand people to get the information you need, but certainly leave your bubble and encourage others to contribute ideas that you don't have.

Getting Input That Counts

- It doesn't matter whether the issue is business or personal. Consider creating a "kitchen cabinet" of friends or colleagues, or an impartial focus group that is as diverse in thought as it is in demographics.

- Clearly present the challenge you face to members of the group.

- Encourage them to brainstorm as quickly as they can. You want a quantity of options, and don't shut anybody down with criticism about the quality of the ideas. You'll weed out the bad ideas later.

- When the ideas stop flowing, ask everybody to come up with two more.

- Then, sort through the list.

What if?

People frequently stall their dreams and their progress by fixating on "what if" scenarios that never happen. The "what if" mindset can and will stop you from achieving anything if you give it too much power, because it so frequently opens you to the fear and uncertainty that undermines your resolve and confidence. I am reluctant to tell you to consider the "what if" consequences without issuing a warning up front. You will want to think through the various scenarios and consequences that could play out with your alternative decision options, but you absolutely should not obsess on the negatives or use them as excuses to chicken out.

There are *always* negatives out there, whether they are visible on the surface or not. There are always bad things that could happen. But if you give power to those bad possibilities, you will never shake anything up. So much greatness is born from confidence in risk-taking and decision-making, but whether you can embrace your potential for excellence depends largely on whether you believe you are the right person to make the decision, carry it out and deal with the fallout – whatever that fallout may be.

You can certainly prepare yourself for potential fallout by running through the "what if" scenarios, and I encourage you to do so. If you look at every option and really question what might happen – good and bad – you will make a sound decision and be prepared for what lies ahead. That kind of prep work should be done in order to keep you on track when things go wrong. However, it is natural for some people to let their minds slip into a negativity or fear loop with these "what ifs" and begin to expect everything to go wrong.

As I said earlier, I'm a strong believer in the Law of Attraction, which says, basically, you manifest what you think. So if you think you're going to have trouble, you're going to have trouble. If you expect success, you'll get it one way or another. But, you also have to back yourself with hard work and intelligence.

The point here is to explore what might happen in order to help you make the best decision, but not to use the negatives as an excuse to be weak or cowardly.

Decide! No, WAIT!

"Act with a surgeon's scalpel, not a dull butcher's knife."

My old boss gave me that bit of advice as I confided that I was contemplating a divorce. His point was that I should make a clean, quick break, rather than making it drawn out and bloody. It was the worst piece advice I have ever received in my life.

I have no idea why I listened. It was the same guy who let the circulation director hike the price of papers in the news racks.

Looking at it now, it seems like such a clinical and simplistic way to approach major decisions. Just act, be decisive and get on with it. In my case, it completely ignored the fact that, as an individual, I am more feeling than analytical in personal decisions. The fallout left me with years of uncertainty and regret. I'd done exactly as he suggested, making the decision to divorce, telling my husband, filing the paperwork and getting on with my life.

What I hadn't done was grieve the marriage, accept the loss and reflect on what it had meant in my life. I was sure the marriage was broken. Sort of. But, my former husband actively pursued me for remarriage for years afterwards, and I always entertained that possibility – even coming close to actually doing it – because I hadn't done my prep work on the front end of the decision. If I'd acted a little more slowly, I would have worked through my ambivalence. I did love him, but it wasn't a solid marriage. I did need to divorce him, no doubt about that, but I needed to do it in a way that was more deliberative and final.

Sometimes, you just know you are making a decision that will haunt you later. When it is personal or emotional, it has a way of hanging on. In those instances, move forward with the confidence and boldness of a strong individual acting in his or her own best interests, but take time to know that you are doing what your soul is calling you to do so that you can minimize the uncertainty or misgivings later. And, don't let others pressure you or influence you to act when you don't feel right acting.

Not every decision has to be analytical or cynical. Sometimes they come from the heart, and when that happens, listen to what your heart is saying. Work it through. Move forward knowing you have not rushed yourself into a judgment that you will not fully embrace later.

Don't Be Impulsive

The day after I gave a speech on risk-taking, I got an e-mail from a woman in the audience who told me I had inspired her to go into work and quit her job. Just like that. Poof! Instant unemployment.

I asked her what she planned to do with her life.

"I don't know," she wrote back. "But I didn't like my job."

I asked her if she had a good nest egg to fall back on.

"Not really," she e-mailed. "I can make it for a month or six weeks without going into my retirement money."

I asked her if she had a lot saved for her retirement.

"Oh, not much at all for someone who is 57. My financial planner told me I am crazy."

Okay, this was not a good experience for me. It shook me to think that someone used something I said to blindly leap off the cliff into the difficulties that most certainly would -- and actually did – come her way. I haven't heard from her in quite a while, and I feel guilty that I haven't written to check in, but I don't want to say anything that will "inspire" her to make another impulsive mistake.

I am always urging people to live their dreams, follow their hearts and take risks. But impulsivity is not your friend. Why would you ditch your livelihood without a plan to sustain yourself? Or dump your life's savings into a business opportunity that you know nothing about? Or get a tattoo because you've had a few drinks and the tattoo parlor is right there? People do those things all the time. A colleague of mine once quit her job on the spot when her boss told her she was "average" in a performance review. It infuriated her. She remained unemployed for a year.

Sure, we live in a fast-paced world where stupid people risk everything without thinking. How many men and women have cheated on their spouses and risked everything, just because of impulse? How many investors have plunged money into bad stocks just because they felt sure they were about to make a killing? We could list thousands of stupid things people do every day just because they act without thinking. They decide on a whim, consequences be damned.

Sure, I tell you to be decisive and not wait for 100 percent certainty, but DO YOUR HOMEWORK!

Decide Not to Decide

You can avoid a decision, you can stall a decision, you can drop the decision completely. But you have to own what you are doing. Denial is cowardly, especially if you may face consequences for your chicken-heartedness later. If you aren't going to do anything, know that you are staying out of it for a reason. Consciously acknowledge what you are doing – and not doing.

If you aren't deciding because you are being a wimp, own it. Say, "I'm not up to this now, so I am not going to do anything about it." Or, "I am not concerned with what might happen if I do nothing. I am staying out of this one," or, "I am too busy right now to deal with this one, so I am going to take a pass."

It's okay to "pull a Scarlett O'Hara." Scarlett's classic line in *Gone With the Wind* was, "I can't think about that right now. If I do, I'll go crazy. I'll think about that tomorrow."

That works. The problem occurs when you keep putting it off. It is too easy to back-burner decisions to the point where they are never addressed. It is also easy to go into denial mode, minimize the problem and neglect to do anything about it. Not taking action is a decision, even if you aren't aware that you are making the decision not to decide.

Just know what you are doing. Or not doing.

Granted, you will likely encounter plenty of opportunities to make decisions that really don't need to be made. Things sometimes take care of themselves, or problems aren't as big as they seem. If you don't have to do anything and don't feel the need to do it, don't do it.

Just know what you are doing – and not doing.

The Weighted Decision Table

Again, the simple pro and con list ignores the reality that few considerations deserve equal weight. For example, you are considering moving across country for a better job. The traditional pro and con list might look like the following:

PROS	CONS
1. Beautiful city 2. Better job 3. Better money 4. Lower cost of living	1. Far away from family 2. Won't be able to help take care of aging parents 3. Will miss friends

Try a weighted formula to help you decide. After each consideration, rate your decision on a scale of 1 to 10 points, with 10 being something extremely important to you. Your chart will look like this:

PROS	POINTS	CONS	POINTS
Beautiful city	8	Far away from family	10
Better job	8	Won't be able to help take care of aging parents	10
Better money	9	Will miss friends	8
Lower Cost of Living	10	Terrible school system	10
TOTAL	35		38

There is also the wildcard factor. Any pro or con can be a wildcard issue that can trump the value of everything else combined. If you really love your aging parents and feel like you need to be there to help care for them, it might not matter if there are a thousand points in the other column.

You Can Handle the Consequences

Decision-making is always an imprecise science. You can seldom predict every possible outcome, but you can move forward with confidence and boldness, knowing you have the ability to be versatile, flexible, strong and able as you encounter any setbacks or obstacles. At some point, you will realize that the power of good decision-making doesn't come from controlling or foreseeing all outcomes, but rather, from the confidence that you can handle the outcome – whatever happens. Good or bad. You are smart and agile. Don't forget it.

Hopefully, you have done the homework to help you ensure a good outcome. But this is real life, and things seldom go as planned. The only thing you can truly plan is your resolve to move forward, regardless of what happens. That means living with the certainty that you will alter your responses to whatever outcomes arise, and face the difficulties head-on.

Get on with it

Okay, you've decided. Great. Act on the decision, do whatever it is you need to do, then get on with things. Endless studies have been done on the second-guessing that arises when we determine how to proceed.

There is a kind of buyer's remorse whenever we make a decision. When you buy a car, you might wonder if you got the right model or if you should have negotiated harder or if you should have hung onto your old car longer. When you find a new home, you wonder if you should have chosen a different neighborhood, price range or color of bricks. You can get buyer's remorse when choosing life partners or jobs or items off a menu. You can second-guess yourself to death, and many people do.

That kind of unease will undermine your effectiveness when it comes to executing your decision and following through. Okay, you have made the decision. How are you going to make it work? Is it necessary to look back? Do you have to bother yourself with thoughts of the choices you didn't make?

Some people will tell you that you should never look back, and that is largely true. But there will be times when you make a decision and begin to travel your path and realize you have made a mistake. How far are you going to travel on the wrong path? Is there a point where you "cut your losses," recalibrate and push for a different outcome?

How many times have you heard someone say, "I got married and I knew I was making a mistake before I even said 'I do.'" Well, why on earth would you move forward with something like that if you knew it wasn't going to work? And if you did make a mistake, how many years would you have to sacrifice before doing something to fix that bad decision? If you are miserable, do something! The other person deserves a happy relationship, too! Whether it is at work or at home, you can make a course correction if the need arises.

I can tell you that you should never regret a decision, and you will get a lot of positive energy in life if you can live without regrets. You did what you thought was the right thing to do. It may have been the right thing at that time, and things may have changed. But if you know you've made a mistake, you shouldn't delude yourself into believing that it will all work out, or that you can force it to work if you give more, or that it doesn't matter, you have to stick by your decision "just because." Should you keep telling yourself you are doing the right thing? Keep wasting time, energy and possibility on something that is not right? Or should you make a change? You have permission to revoke or change a decision! Just don't give up before it is time to give up.

Deciding to Decide

Can we teach ourselves to do the lists, deliberate, then act? Is it necessary to deliberate to death? The big leap comes when you learn that a mistake will not be the end of life as you know it. Senior executives can usually rattle off a list of this or that decision that went south or was poorly timed, but their success wasn't built solely on their ability to make great decisions. It was built on their ability to make great decisions *and* recover from the ones that weren't so great.

Nobody hits a home run every single time. Home run king Babe Ruth also had the major league record for striking out. It's all about the recovery.

You wouldn't be where you are if you did not have some knowledge of how to make decisions. But if you want to function in a rapidly changing environment, you need the confidence jolt that helps you to make a decision and get on with it.

I do not advocate snap decisions or recklessness. Get your information. Do your research. Talk to people. Deliberate. Talk to more people. Deliberate a little more. But then, ACT WHEN YOU NEED TO ACT!

It is highly unlikely that any decision you make will result in your being such an abject failure that you wind up homeless, eating out of garbage cans and unemployable until the day you die, so stop acting like that's what you will face if you goof. A big decision is a big challenge. It is not cancer. Reserve your worry for the things that matter, like family, health and life decisions. Business is important, but a bad decision will not kill you. Don't make yourself so insecure that you lose your effectiveness.

How do you reprogram yourself to have the confidence to know you will make the right decision?

Well, consider your track record. You've made so many decisions over the course of your lifetime. How many of them were huge mistakes? Probably not that many. So, know that you've decided well in the past and you will decide well in the future.

In my 20s, I was setting up a pattern of making decisions, then trying to quickly reverse them. I am so lucky I had a boss who sat me down and told me he'd observed what I was doing. There were little things, like deciding I wanted to move out of my apartment at the beach. I put a deposit on a place, then changed my mind on that. Then I transferred from the city desk over to features, then wanted back on the city desk.

"Just make a decision and stick with it," my editor said.

As if it were that easy!

My big surprise was, it really was that easy.

I did what he said. I made decisions. I stuck with them. I stopped fearing mistakes because I knew I could handle whatever came out of my choices. There have been good calls and bad calls, but everything has pretty much worked out okay. I certainly got the kind of life and success I wanted to create. Actually, I got way more than that. I am proof that you can train yourself to be a decision-maker – even when you hate decision-making.

Decisions are not hard for me at all anymore, and haven't been – ever since he gave me that pep talk. That doesn't mean I don't make a decision and then have a course correction. I do that all the time. If something isn't working out, I know to tweak the decision or go ahead and cut my losses. But I am not afraid to try something different, to take an enormous risk and just charge forward knowing that I have what it takes to make things work out in the end.

That's all you need to know. That you are smart enough to make sure that, ultimately, it will all work out. Don't give energy to the negativity. Stop worrying about so many what-ifs. It's not going to kill you.

You'll make good decisions, and you'll make bad ones. But you'll get to where you need to go. It'll all work out. You are way too brilliant for anything less.

Decision Checklist

As you evaluate your decision, ask yourself:

- What will this decision accomplish?
- How does it fit with your overall vision and mission?
- Who does the decision affect? Have you explored options with them? Are they on board?
- Does this decision really need to be made?
- Does it need to be made by you?
- How much time do you truly have? Do you have the luxury of waiting a month or two months or even a year?
- What is the worst thing that will happen if you delay the decision?
- What if you don't act at all?
- If you need to make a decision, make it. You know the cliché: The decision not to decide is a decision.
- What is making you feel uneasy?

- What's the real risk involved?
- What is the most predictable alternative? Unpredictable? Practical? Impractical? Popular? Unpopular? Safe? Outrageous?
- What do others expect you to do?
- How likely is it that the worst-case scenario will play out?
- What are your checkpoints where you will re-evaluate and consider a course correction?
- Do you have the support of the people above you? Below you? What do they say?
- Are you basing the decision on substance rather than popularity?
- Have you brainstormed with others?
- Can the decision be delayed?

It is important to write down your problem analysis because it helps you to clarify your thinking and it gives you a written record of what needs to be done, and what you have tried. Since some issues will drag out for months or even years, it will be helpful to have reminders in place so you will know what has worked and what hasn't.

It's NOT About Balance. It's About Choices.

"Imagine life as a game in which you are juggling five balls in the air. You name them - work, family, health, friends, and spirit - and you're keeping all of these in the air. You will soon understand that work is a rubber ball. If you drop it, it will bounce back. But the other four balls - family, health, friends, and spirit are made of glass. If you drop one of these, they will be irrevocably scuffed, marked, nicked, damaged, or even shattered. They will never be the same."

Brian Dyson, *CEO of Coca Cola Enterprises from 1959-1994*

Work. Life. Balance. Work. Life. Balance. We've all heard those words so much it's as if they have merged into a simple mantra which, if we repeat it enough, we will manifest. "Work. Life. Balance." "Work. Life. Balance." "Work. Life. Balance."

Poof!

Look at her! See that career woman climb that company ladder! Look how happy her marriage is! My, aren't her children beautiful, successful and happy! She still has time to cook gourmet recipes, clean house and have great sex! Not only that, she still plays tennis, too!

It doesn't work like that.

It takes work to grow into your identity and balance yourself out by making decisions that let *you* define success and failure, rather than being ruled by traditional expectations or guilt. *That* is how you achieve life balance. You do it consciously and on your own terms.

Know your priorities and know where they rank. You've got to drop the ball somewhere, and it's time to choose where yours will drop. That is the first step in balancing your soul.

Are You Making the Right Choices?

	Always	Usually	Sometimes	Rarely	Never
I have enough alone time.					
I know what my priorities are.					
If something is important in my life, it gets the time it deserves.					
I say no to other people and assignments to make time for what matters to me.					
I lose time going to events that I won't enjoy just because I think I should be there.					
I spend time with people I won't enjoy just because I can't say no.					
I feel guilty about the amount of quality time I spend with my significant other.					
I feel guilty about the amount of time I spend with my children.					
I have enough going on in my life that I am a well-rounded, interesting person.					
Business travel interferes with my home life.					

	Always	Usually	Sometimes	Rarely	Never
I get to spend the amount of time I want to spend with community, church or volunteer efforts.					
I have enough time to do kind things for other people.					
I am in charge of my schedule.					
I know what my life priorities are and constantly make sure I am taking care of them.					
I feel like I am putting the right amount of energy into housekeeping and getting the right results.					
I delegate well in order to make more quality time for the priorities that matter.					
I have a lot of fun in my life.					
I am always running to get things done.					
At the end of the day, I feel "caught up" with things.					
I am a good example of a person making the right choices toward a priority-driven life.					

I get so amused by the importance people give to the notion of work life balance. Like, once we get it right, we all let out a nice, long Zen *ohm* and all will be well. Balance implies some sort of time/effort equity that few ever achieve in life. I certainly don't, and I don't even have a husband or children to worry about.

I remember former cable television senior executive Gayle Greer showing me how she learned to balance her soul. As a working single parent, she traveled about 80 percent of the time when her son was growing up. He seldom came along. One day, he asked if he could schedule time for her to meet with a couple of coaches who wanted to talk to her about college scholarship possibilities for him. "It blew me away," she said. "College? I hadn't even thought about it. I wasn't living in the present. I was so intensely holding on to whatever it was, keeping all the balls up in the air. Then it dawned on me, this kid is leaving." That changed her forever. She never missed one of her son's football games after that.

Our lives move so quickly that it seems like we are powerless over our schedules. But, we're not. You may think you are too important or too busy or too stretched, but you have got to make time so you don't lose your "self. " If you think you can't, or you can't do it right now, you are wrong. If someone you loved were suddenly in a life or death situation, your current schedule would screech to a halt and you would know what really matters.

Balance is about identity. It's knowing who you are and what matters most so that you honor your priorities in the way you want and need to honor them. We sacrifice so much of ourselves to things that don't matter.

The mantra isn't "Work life balance." It's, "I know what matters and I honor that truth."

Checking in With Yourself

It's not a question of balance. It's a question of choices. What matters to *you*? Don't think about what others expect of you in your life, but what *you* expect of yourself. Ultimately, you are no good to anybody if you are not good to yourself. So...

When you die, what are the three things you want people to say about you?

How much of your current life is focused on honoring those characteristics that you will ultimately hold most dear?

Are you living a fulfilled life or not? Why or why not?

What do you want to do to more fully enjoy your life?

Now, imagine your obituary. What will matter more when all is said and done? That you were a good workaholic or that you were a whole and complete person? Write the first four paragraphs of your obituary.

Housework Can Be Delegated. Life Can't.

I have no idea how you pull it off. How many e-mails, voice mails, phone calls or faxes did you deal with today? How many meetings and conference calls? Lunch appointments, calendar shuffles and "emergency" interruptions?

I sure hope you made time to pick up the kids, do the wash, clean the kitchen and help with homework, because if you didn't, you must be a terrible mother, a horrible housekeeper and a really lame wife.

I'm just kidding. I often am hired to help corporate women and men deal with those famous "work-life balance" issues, and I constantly tell them that they a) can't do it all, b) should stop trying, and c) need to cut themselves some slack. More than anything, they need to stop wallowing in guilt and start making changes that will free up their time and brain cells.

Who are you, anyway? You aren't a robot or Superwoman or June Cleaver. You might be able to do two things at once, maybe three. But you can't do ten, and the way this world operates, you feel inadequate if you can't. If you are a star in your career but you drop the ball for even one minute when it comes to perfect performance at home, you feel like a complete failure.

Years ago, I was working on the most exhaustive investigative reporting project I had ever undertaken. It lasted for ten months, and the last two months of the project just about killed me. I was meeting with sources from the state attorney general's office in the basement of a McDonald's restaurant. Staking out the mayor's office. Dealing with what appeared to be our local Watergate. Numerous city officials were fired and criminally investigated.

Because of that work, I was nominated for the Pulitzer prize – twice. But, in the middle of it, several friends stopped by my house before we went for the usual Friday night dinner out. Most of the house looked presentable. But, I have to admit, I'd shoved a lot of piles of paperwork and other "stuff" into the junk room because I hadn't had time to deal with them.

I don't know whether my now ex-husband thought he was being funny or if he was deliberately being passive aggressive, but he called everyone together in the hallway and said, "You've got to see this." He opened the door to the junk room and exposed my mess.

In the midst of my greatest professional success, I'd been outed as a failed housekeeper, which somehow translated into a failed wife in my mind.

Granted, I have evolved a bit since that happened. I know I can't do everything, and the first thing that is going to give is housework. I've got a relationship and family and work and life and I will take care of those priorities before I clear the pile off my desk.

Housework can be delegated, but life can't. Remember that.

Balance? We don't get that kind of equilibrium very often. One priority often trumps another. It has to. If you waste energy trying to be great at everything, you are good at nothing.

What Matters Most?

My first day on the job at *The Miami Herald* was an absolute shock. My boss had really laid everything on nice and thick as she courted me in the hiring process, but the minute I arrived for my first day at work, she informed me that I'd be working some weeknights, every Saturday day shift and, gee, when I wasn't working until 12, I'd be expected to hang until at least about 8 — even if I was done with my work.

I went there when I was only in the third week of my marriage. At a time when I should have been enjoying life as a newlywed, I was being tested to see how loyal I was to the whims of a newspaper with insatiable demands.

It didn't seem fair. My work was important to me — *extremely* important to me. I was passionate about it, and I delivered huge front-page stories. But I had a relationship to tend to. I'd just moved to town and wanted to get out and make friends and learn about my new city. I'd always turn my stories in on time — at 6:30 p.m. — but that didn't matter. *Nobody* left that early. Nobody.

So there I would sit, watching the clock and wondering when I could leave. I was done with my work. Other reporters were turning in their stories late, so why couldn't I benefit from my always on-time performance and go home to my husband?

A few weeks into my tenure there, editors from *The Palm Beach Post* invited me to lunch and offered me a job with better assignments, better money and much better hours. I turned them down, thinking I owed something to *The Herald.* The editor of *The Post* told me that editors at *The Herald* wouldn't think twice about cutting me if it benefited them. I didn't believe them.

A month later — just days before Christmas — the managing editor came to our bureau and announced the paper was shutting the Palm Beach operation down. Half of us would be spared, half would not. I survived the cut. The ones who didn't make it were the veterans who didn't have the same paranoia that us newcomers felt as we tried to impress our bosses. I thought about what that editor at *The Post* had said, and it was so very true.

I was transferred to another bureau and worked weekends and wasted more hours just sitting there late because my bosses wanted me to be part of the team. The politics of those offices were so brutal that I routinely saw one editor setting up the next in hopes of getting rid of a potential competitor. The entire time I worked there, I was on edge. I had no time for my husband or myself.

My first anniversary was approaching, and I knew they would never let me out in time for a celebratory dinner. I knew it. So I called in sick. I had to take a sick day in order to make sure I could go out at 7 p.m. with my husband.

When I finally took a vacation, we flew to Greece for two weeks. I still have the journal where I was wrestling with the pulls of my work versus the true priorities in my life — God, relationship, family, friends and humanity. I closed it saying, "When I die, it will mean far more to me to have people say that I loved and was loved than that I really knew how to write a 12-inch news story. I need to learn to live my life for the big picture." All that wisdom, and I was just 28 years old. Notice work wasn't even on the list. It was important to me, but it wasn't central to my being. I came home from that trip and started sending resumes out. A month later, I was gone.

That awakening stayed with me and centered me whenever work would start to take over my life. Work is work. It is exciting and challenging and mandatory. But, it is work.

So as you start to contemplate the balance issue, ask yourself what matters most in your life.

What are the five or six "pulls" that you have to honor?

What does each priority mean to your world?

If you only had one week on earth, how would you spend your time?

What really matters to you?

The "What matters most?" question will always serve to give you perspective and help you decide how to divvy up your time. Some people write a personal mission statement that incorporates their priorities so they can always check in easily to see if they have veered off course. Before you wear yourself out trying to juggle everything, go within to make sure you are juggling what really matters to you.

Go Ahead. Just Drop the Ball.

Soon after *Hard Won Wisdom* was released, my insurance agent asked me to save her a signed copy. When I dropped it by her office, she thumbed through it and said, "Maybe this will show me how to juggle all these balls I have in the air."

I looked at her and said, "The secret to juggling is to let some of the balls drop."

Simple enough. It is so important to know what matters most in your life. Once you have that list of what really counts, you will see that you are wasting time on activities and "pulls" that keep you from the things that really move your soul.

First, look at your calendar. How are you spending your time? How much time are you handing over to tasks and people that don't hold value to you? It is easy to hand over your time to obligations that are really meaningless to your life.

Evaluating Your Time Drains

We all wind up sacrificing time to duties or people that don't ultimately matter in life's big picture. Take a few moments to look at your time drains and evaluate them to see whether some of them can be minimized or eliminated.

Give each time drain a necessity score of 1 to 5, with 1 being something that is absolutely mandatory and necessary, and 5 being something you could slack off on.

Time Drains	Necessity Score 1-5	Hours / Week It Takes	Can This Time Drain Be Minimized?	Can You Just Say No to This?
1.				
2.				
3.				
4.				
5.				
6.				
7.				
8.				
9.				
10.				
11.				
12.				
13.				
14.				
15.				

Worst Time Drains	What I Can Do About It

Conscious Scheduling

There was a time when I spent almost every lunch hour networking and trying to build my business. I thought it was necessary, a part of the job. But I learned something. **Time is too precious to hand over to people you don't especially like or to waste on things you don't especially want to do.** I know how important it is to network, but I got much, much smarter at it. Instead of doing five lunches a week, I devoted half a day to it. I didn't waste time driving downtown for lunch every day. I'd meet someone for breakfast, then someone for coffee, then drop by someone's office, then do lunch. I would do a week's worth of networking at once. After a while, I became much more discriminating about whom I would even network with. It's amazing how much time I had once I took control over that.

You also have to be an expert at organizing yourself because there are a million distractions and "pulls" that will keep you from doing the things you really want or need to do. E-mail is a great example. What a great idea that was when it was first invented! Now, I hate it. A lot of people do. We now get hundreds of them every day and have no time for our *real* work. It's absurd, and so is the cell phone. We used to have lives. Now we can be reached anytime, anywhere. We feel compelled to constantly check in to see what is happening. We don't fully engage in conversations because we are trying to check the Blackberry or Treo out of the corner of our eye.

We used to worry about balancing work and family demands. Now we can't even balance ourselves.

It is because we have not realized that we have the power to set good boundaries that give us room to live and breathe. Who is more balanced, the person who checks e-mail while driving in traffic or the person who only checks e-mail once a day? The once-a-day person has set boundaries that create a healthy life.

Then there are those periods when everything is happening and there truly is no time to stop and take stock of anything. I know about this because the speaking industry has some peak seasons that can really exhaust me. One time, I was so stretched that I hadn't had a day off in six weeks. I was tired and grumpy and one-dimensional. I took out my PDA and opened up my calendar. Two weeks out, there was a Friday with nothing scheduled. I wrote in the word "OFF." And that is when I learned the secret that, if you block a day off like that, it does not exist. All of my appointments had to flow around it.

I do that all the time now — just keep a day for myself. It is healthy.

So, as you juggle so many balls in the air, realize that you are the one who decides what you are going to keep juggling and what you are going to drop. Stop killing yourself.

Grading Your Life. How are you meeting your life's needs? Use this chart to score what you are currently doing with your life. Score 1-5 for priorities (with 1 being highest) and A-F for grades on how you are achieving them.

	Priority 1-5	Grade	What You Are Doing Right	What You Are Doing Wrong
Professional				
Relationship				
Parenting				
Other Family Obligations				
Friends / Social				
Health				
Spirituality				
Appearance				
Growth and Development				
Learning				
Recreation				
Community Service				

Balancing Your Life.

Now figure out what isn't working for you and what you are going to do to change things.

	Priority	What You Want to Change	Action Steps
Professional			
Relationship			
Parenting			
Other Family Obligations			
Friends / Social			
Health			
Spirituality			
Appearance			
Growth and Development			
Learning			
Recreation			
Community Service			

The Firewall Between Your Time and Theirs

I once received an e-mail from an executive's Blackberry, inquiring about my speaking at an event she was hosting. Get this: She was sending that e-mail while she was getting a root canal. I am not kidding. Janet Johnston now wins the Oscar for Best Performance by a Type-A Personality.

It gets better. In the middle of all that, she was summoned to talk to some government official for the routine meeting about her *au pair*. She had to get out of the oral surgeon's chair, cotton in mouth, and make the appearance.

Janet!

I love her. Love her energy, love her vibe, love her indomitable ways. But, Sister has *got* to chill. In this balance dilemma, it is so important that you build up the personal firewall that will protect you and your time. It is way too easy for work to intrude on personal and family time because a) companies are more demanding than ever b) it is so easy for work contacts to reach us at all times c) we often feel a need to demonstrate unlimited loyalty in the line of duty d) we get a little too wrapped up in what we are doing.

Knock it off, or you will go crazy. You have the right to reserve time for yourself and your family. If you feel that pressure is on you to be available 24/7, talk to your boss about making some adjustments. Employers are sensitive to the balance issue these days because it is costing them money when employees leave.

Make it clear that your job is important to you and that you are committed to succeeding with the company. But you need to have a firewall that gives you time with your family so that you don't raise a bunch of drug addicts and juvenile delinquents, or wind up e-mailing people from your Blackberry when you are getting a root canal.

"Our lives are a mixture of different roles. Most of us are doing the best we can to find whatever the right balance is . . . For me, that balance is family, work, and service." Hillary Clinton

How Do You Do all of That and Raise a Family?

I used to hate it when editors would have me ask women of power the question, "How do you do all of this *and* raise a family?" I thought the question was insulting, especially since I was never told to ask it of men. But after talking with so many women who are trying to do it all, that remains the question. How do women do such extraordinary things without letting their home lives fall apart?

I hear so much anxiety over this one issue. The guilt women (especially) feel over having to travel or work late or miss events is depleting, consuming and powerful. They feel that they are missing so much, that their children will resent them, that others will judge them. That they are doing things all wrong.

I am constantly asked about balance issues. The reality is that there is no issue of balance; it's all about imbalance. It's about making the imbalance work so you can succeed professionally while raising children who are not juvenile delinquents — and so you can avoid losing your mind in the process. Women always are running to keep up with the demands. Despite their efforts to do it all, they are tortured by guilt because, let's face it: They can never do enough.

Is it selfish to want a career?

Is it selfish to want to be with your children?

Is it selfish to want ten minutes to yourself?

Is it selfish to want a little bit of everything?

So many of the young mothers I meet describe a frenetic pace they must sustain as parents and professionals. I just flew back from a speech in Chicago and was almost mowed down at the newsstand counter by a woman who pleaded with the clerk, "Where is there a store that sells children's toys?" I hear about that so much – that when a woman leaves town for work, the guilt is so immense that she has to desperately find something to bring back in her suitcase.

Do men feel as guilty as women about not pulling off the perfect life balancing act?

Are they compelled to be equal players, help with the housework and children, plus carry half the guilt when work keeps them from participating in something personal? Thoughts?

I interviewed more than 50 of the most successful women in American business for my book, *The NEW Woman Rules*. Nearly two thirds of the women who are mothers have husbands who are stay-at-home dads. Nationally, the Bureau of Labor Statistics reports that just one in five fathers are stay-at-home dads, so these numbers of senior executive women with Mr. Mom at home are startling.

What does it mean when these senior women choose this option? Does it prove that the old model was right? That the senior executive needs someone at home running the household and taking care of the kids in order to make everything work?

I think it suggests that running a household and raising a family are such demanding challenges that every parent needs all the help she or he can get. And that those who make it to senior leadership are in a better position to pay for that option because they have the bigger paychecks.

What would happen to those national statistics if every family could afford financially to choose that option? Senior leadership is a demanding world, but is it any more demanding than a world where a woman works two back-breaking jobs to pay her family's bills? There are a lot of women who would just love to have that kind of support at home.

Are you bearing the primary responsibility for housekeeping?

For childcare?

For cooking?

How does your mate pitch in?

How could he or she help you more?

How do you feel about this? Does this arrangement work for you?

Have you talked about it? What kind of response have you gotten?

Can you get more help from your mate?

Can you afford to hire more help?

What can you do as a team to make this situation work better for you?

Stop Feeling Selfish. It is YOUR Life.

There is sometimes an assumption that women who climb to the highest reaches of the professional world have hardened into being selfish, not selfless, in their quest for power. The stereotype is that the professional woman thinks she can "have it all" – but can't—and willingly swaps mommy time to keep moving up.

The stereotype is wrong. I am convinced of that because of the way everything stops when I bring up the subject of family in the interviews. If you wonder what matters most to these women, ask about their passion for their work. Then ask if they have children. The tone of voice always changes. It softens. The women open up. Maybe they can't always be with their family in body, but they are always there in heart. They have felt their share of guilt for not being around every minute of the day, but you can just see that they really have been there, just the same.

I hope their children feel that.

These mothers function in a hard-driving, often-unforgiving level of the business world that constantly foists expectations on them. What is so interesting is that those expectations seem so insignificant when you contrast them to what these women expect of themselves—as mothers. They truly want to do right by their children.

But these serious questions of balance don't apply solely to women with family obligations. I interviewed Walgreens Vice President and Chief Marketing Officer Kim Feil, who showed how easy it is for those of us who don't have children to become so consumed by work that all other signs of personal identity are lost. The demands that children and family make of mothers are so immediate that balance decisions are always right there in full view. But when you are not being pulled on by family priorities that so obviously need and deserve your attention, it can be all too easy to slip into the self-neglect that Feil experienced. Life becomes work, work, work. You don't have much else to talk about with outsiders, or to think about when you go home. The good news is that you can wake up to the fact that there is a full, exciting, colorful world out there, just waiting for you to make the decision to embrace it.

Also, this is 2010. Men have taken a *much* more active role in their home lives, not just because of fairness, but because they are beginning to tap into what matters to their own hearts and souls. There is no stigma to saying that "soccer calls," and they are starting to do that. But, I still see a lot less guilt when they put business demands first. Maybe that will change. The good thing is that men are choosing to be involved.

I get perspective on the life balance issue when I think of one of the newspapers where I worked. I worked very hard as a reporter, but I noticed something about my job.

If I took a long lunch hour, the paper still came out. If I went on vacation, the paper still came out. If I switched jobs and moved away, the paper still came out. It came out every day, whether I was there or not. So many of us delude ourselves into thinking we are so indispensable that we must make great personal sacrifice to save the institution. But there aren't a lot of situations in which the business will sink because we take some time to ourselves.

And, forgive the heresy here, but it is only business. Life—in all of its glory—is far more important than the immediate task at hand.

"One of the symptoms of an approaching nervous breakdown is the belief that one's work is terribly important."
– Bertrand Russell, British Philosopher

I recently went to a small dinner party where one guest was someone who is in the Fortune 10 group of the most powerful women in business. She was warm, accessible and kind. But she didn't have much to offer our conversation about life balance except her regrets that she has no time to golf or hang out or do any of the things she would really like to do.

I asked, "Why don't you just do some of those things so you don't burn out?"

She looked at me like I just didn't get it. "I have the weight of the world on my shoulders," she said. She said it very dramatically, and I could tell she meant it. Then she said, "When I accepted this job, I made a commitment to the company and the stockholders. I have no other option."

Truth is, I didn't get it. Why would anyone choose to give up life for work? Even a temporary sacrifice like that is too much because, living in just that one dimension, you will challenge your physical and mental health to the point where you stop living in a colorful world. We've all seen colleagues humbled by heart attacks and strokes, or even extended bouts of depression. The one thing I think we are all called upon to do is live in the moment. Live a vibrant, colorful life in the now.

I think of two veteran journalists who loved my newspaper so much that they had their ashes encased in the walls after they died. Instead of having their ashes spread in the glorious Rocky Mountains around them, they chose the newspaper lobby? It said everything about what the paper meant to them and, probably, what they thought they meant to the paper. But, theirs was a sad choice, because decades after their deaths, people didn't care about who they were, what they'd done or what they meant to the history of the newspaper. It was a bit of a joke that there were ashes in the wall. And, aggravating the insult, when the paper was moved into a new building, the remains were removed and buried in a cemetery. Management didn't even extend the courtesy of letting them make the move with everybody else.

You can give and give and give and give, and the business will take and take and take and take. In the end, who you are matters so much more than what you did.

The business won't love you back.

When You Have Too Much To Do and No Time To Do It

Prioritize and organize. Have a "to do" list for every day, and try to get through it. Make tomorrow's list at the end of your workday and star the items that must be done first. That way you hit the ground running.

Focus. Know what your major goals are for the week and don't get distracted.

Tackle the hard assignments first – and get them done early. That frees up the rest of your time for less taxing assignments that can be done without worrying about the big assignment you haven't started.

Save the easy assignments for the time of day when you aren't at your best. That could be phone calls or e-mails or whatever doesn't require your full brain power.

Minimize socializing. You'll save a lot of time if you stop yakking around the water cooler, instant messaging or texting friends or going for unnecessary or long lunches.

Clean up your mess. Clutter makes it harder to do your job.

Quit procrastinating. Just do the hard or unpleasant tasks you have to do first and don't lose time worrying about them.

Set deadlines. Know how long each assignment should take, and try to complete it on schedule.

Manage your e-mail. Separate your work e-mails from the jokes and personal ones. Look at e-mail only at specific times of the day.

Don't get stuck in the mud. If things aren't clicking with what you are doing, either take a break or switch to another assignment and come back to it when your mind is refreshed.

Use your commute to your advantage. Do work or read when you are on mass transit. If you are in the car, listen to tapes. Have work with you when you are waiting for meetings in other offices.

Schedule alone time. Clear your mind and focus on what you need to do and how you intend to do it. Or do nothing. Let your mind and body rest.

Have smart meetings. Have an agenda, and send it around before the meeting. If you have a choice, use it to decide which meetings you will attend. Handle what you can in e-mails and conference calls, but when you meet, don't let things drag on endlessly.

Delegate. Don't be proud or stupid about doing what other people are able to do. You don't have to do it all, you just have to see that it gets done right. That goes for career work and housework.

Return phone calls during lunch. Leave a voice message; that way, you spend one minute instead of ten connecting.

Know what counts. Few people will ever remember which meetings you missed, but your children and significant other will never forget.

Consider your timing. Maybe you would rather jump off the fast track while your children are young or some other priority is calling you.

Remember…

- Forget "balance." Know your priorities and honor them.
- Too much stress comes from too little organization. Don't "over-schedule" yourself, but use task lists and goals to keep you focused on what really matters in your life.
- Set boundaries. Say no.

- Let things go in order to preserve relationships and sanity. The place won't shut down and the world will not end if you leave early or do a few minimums.

- You perform better when you are a whole person.

- It's not about the quantity of hours you put in. It is about the QUALITY of the hours you work.

- Always remember: Your job will not love you back.

- You have the power to create time. Just schedule it in. Mark a day as "off" and it does not exist for anyone but you.

It's Only Stuff

Recently, my dear friend Jayne abruptly quit her job and hired a company to catalog, price and sell everything she owns at an estate sale so she can move across country to be with her daughter and grandchildren. It was an "Everything Must Go" moment, because what did not sell was going straight to Goodwill. Everything.

The day before the sale, I walked through her home and was amazed that everything from lamps to old school notebooks to knives and forks had a pricetag. When it was over, all of her "stuff" was worth $1,700, of which she kept $1,100. All that stuff. Eleven hundred dollars. Right now, work crews are painting and recarpeting her townhouse, and she is going to unload that, too, instead of holding out until the market rebounds. Note here that a house is also part of your "stuff."

I have watched this woman work in one of the most stress-filled work environments I have ever seen. Her accounting job *demanded* workaholism. When we'd talk on the phone, she was exhausted and out of breath because of too many cigarettes and not enough sleep. I had long thought that job would kill her.

But the moment came when she realized she was here in Florida and the people she loved and needed to be near were all in California. Her daughter's home had a spare apartment in the back. She was wanted there.

Her things were here. Isn't it interesting to see how hard we work to have a place to put our things?

Jayne's "Great Unloading" stands as one of the most empowering I have ever witnessed because she let go of the "things" she was supposed to have in order to live a comfortable life and suddenly, she was free. "Stuff" anchored her to her rut. It anchors all of us.

The notion of leaving my stuff behind hit me when I was in my early 20s and moving out of my first apartment. Everything I owned was boxed up and I looked at the tower of cardboard cartons and thought, "I could walk away from all of this stuff and never miss any of it." Instead of learning from that revelation, I kept amassing more stuff. I scan the room around me now and see so much stuff that I don't need. I need this house just so my stuff has a home.

So many people are so frantic about having the money to hang onto what they have. Maybe the lesson from Jayne is that we are hanging onto the wrong things. If we let go of our belongings and grab onto what really matters in life, we can have so much more while needing so much less. If you suddenly don't need the big house, its contents, the big electric bill, the big water bill for the big yard… what do you need? Not much.

It's only stuff.

1. How much of your life is devoted to maintaining the "stuff" you have amassed?

2. How much stuff do you need?

3. How would your life change if you stopped letting your possessions own you? What if you decided you didn't need to have so much?

4. What matters more than your things? Health? Free time? Family? Make your list of your most important valuables.

5. Could you walk away from your stuff like Jayne did?

6. If you did, would your life be better or worse?

7. What really matters to you?

8. What are the eight most expendable material possessions that cost you the most to support?

   1.

   2.

   3.

   4.

   5.

   6.

   7.

   8.

There is no crime in possessing. The crime occurs when you are owned by what you possess.

Live NOW, Not Later

I don't especially like to watch myself getting older, but there is good news:

1. No matter how old I get, Vicki Smith will always be older than me. She just turned 70, one day before my 49th birthday. That was comforting.

2. If I have to age, I can be like Vicki and not get old.

I met this great woman a few years back when I was working on my novel, *Mermaid Mambo.* Vicki first started performing as a mermaid at Weeki Wachee back in 1957 and resumed her mermaid career at the Central Florida theme park in the 1990s. Vicki helped me to understand the magic of the spring and the wonder of the historic mermaids.

The first time I went tubing down the river with Vicki and the other mermaids, I watched as the then-67-year-old woman climbed a tree, grabbed a rope swing, let out a yell and flew through the air to the river, landing with a spectacular splash. I thought to myself, "I want to be like her when I grow up." So much heart. So much spirit. So much life.

I will now insert photo of Vicki swinging from a tree branch and making monkey noises.

Okay, so about the 70th birthday thing. Vicki wanted to keep it low- key, but she wasn't about to let the day pass without proper commemoration. I will now post the photo of the tattoo Vicki got after consuming a few martinis in Ybor City in Tampa. She put it near her ankle because, she says, she didn't want it anywhere that might have a wrinkle.

"Who wants a wrinkled tattoo?" she asked me. "Name anybody who wrinkles at the ankles."

"An elephant," I answered.

She rolled her eyes.

We went kayaking and I made her show that "tatt" to every person kayaking, canoeing or swimming that we encountered on the river. I told one woman that Vicki had always dreamed of being a Weeki Wachee mermaid, so on her 70th birthday, she decided to get the tattoo. The woman told Vicki to hold onto her dream and apply at the park. Maybe

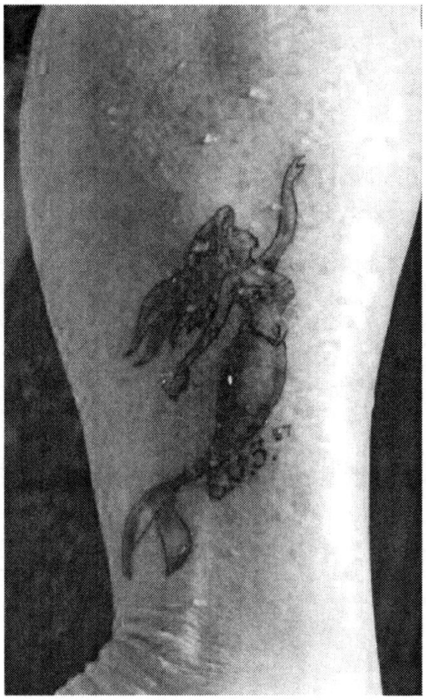

The Tatt

they'd take her! Maybe she could really be a mermaid! Vicki thanked the lady she and promised to call the park to apply.

I am going to start telling people she got the tatt for her *eightieth* birthday. I don't think it'll tick her off because people will then tell her how she doesn't look anywhere near 80.

Do you think you live life "in the moment?" Why or why not?

How much energy do you lose to worrying about the future?

How much energy do you sacrifice to thinking about the past?

What are you going to do to enjoy today?

Do you savor every bite of a meal? Take time to enjoy the expressions on the faces of your loved ones? Relish the sound of beautiful music?

How do you live mindfully?

Do you need to make any changes? What do you think that will mean to your life?

Ten Minutes of Mindfulness

A woman once told me that she'd had a revelation during a therapy session: She wasn't spending *any* time in the present. None. She was either fretting about the past or worrying about the future. She was always distracted from what she was doing.

Her therapist suggested she start by spending ten minutes a day consciously "in the moment."

I looked at her and asked, "You don't already spend ten minutes in the moment every day?"

"No," she said.

"Not even during sex?"

"No."

"Well, that would be the ten minutes I'd start with," I said, laughing She cracked up.

The notion of living in the moment was so foreign to her that even focusing for ten minutes was a challenge. Books have been written on this. The act of conscious living in the moment is called "mindfulness." I just call it "living." Of course, most of us live wildly distracted lives, pulled by what we have to do for work and family, by the technology that is constantly delivering news or messages in an instant, called by our cell phones or webcams or whatever. With all of these "pulls," it's pretty exhausting just waking up in the morning. We're always thinking about something else.

That's not living.

When you are in the shower, is your head busy thinking about something else or are you *feeling* the warmth of the water as it washes over you? When you are walking with a friend or loved one, are you so busy talking about something else that you forget to breathe in the joy that comes by walking outdoors with someone you care about? When you give your child a bath, are you connecting with your child's heart and enjoying that moment, or are you taking care of the chore while planning something else in your head?

Almost all of us have serious problems living right now. I do. I have to catch myself and bring myself back into the moment – otherwise, I stop living a human experience and become a breathing version of a multi-tasking, multi-function computer. I can't tell you how many times I've been on the phone with someone I care about while checking my e-mail or looking something up on the Internet. The worst thing is, the phone call is *not* boring me. Technology has turned me into an overstimulated information consumer who is always one click away from satisfaction. I am definitely not alone. Can you imagine how many times I am doing that on the phone when the other person is doing the very same thing? We are both having phone conversations, but neither one of us is even there!

Two nights ago, I was walking through the restaurant after finishing dinner. I noticed glowing cell phones and Blackberries at six of the ten tables I passed. In some cases, more than one device was in use at a single table. These people were not at business dinners. They were out with friends and family. And instead of enjoying their meals and each other, they were connected to something or someone somewhere else.

Definitely not living in the now.

What's Wrong With Our Attention Spans?

What's wrong with our attention spans? We don't have them! There is a thriving research industry on "Short Attention Span Syndrome" and "Wandering Attention Span" because people are so distracted, they have trouble getting things done.

This is especially problematic for young people who head off to college and don't have the discipline to focus on what they have to do in order to succeed in school. They are now urged to set study schedules and routines, choose study partners who will help them focus on their study goals, study in environments that are free of distractions, and "reward" themselves when they have successfully focused.

I feel like such an old lady. All I had to do to focus when I was in college was go to the library. But how can kids focus in the library when there is free wi-fi that can take them into a whole other universe? This is so hard on young people because they have grown up texting and web surfing. They are so versed in the wonders of technology that they have trouble sitting still and studying.

Even us dinosaurs who don't have mile-a-minute texting thumbs have gotten so immersed in technology that we are leaving the present moment behind.

The distractions we all have are compelling and addicting. This world moves so fast, and the frenetic pace we are forced to maintain winds us up to the point where we can't let go of our stresses. Our world has gone neurotic, and that has robbed us of the simplicity of just "being" here on this Earth. We have to keep up with e-mail and voicemail and Facebook and Twitter and the news and blogs. We are no longer connected to our inner circle of friends – we are connected to people we haven't even thought about for decades, and communicating with them is robbing us of time and energy.

Throw in the fact that people are frantic about debt and foreclosures and job security and retirement and natural disasters and the demise of society at the hands of our politicians and, well, you get it. Most people spend all their time living in their heads, immersed in "something else." They sacrifice the present moment without giving it a thought.

Is that what you do? Is that something you want to change? It takes conscious effort to begin living consciously.

Fortunately, there are exercises that can begin the process. Buddhism is rooted in mindfulness, and meditation is founded on the simplest technique that you can practice and master.

EXERCISE: Breathe in. Breathe out.

Find a quiet, comfortable place and have a seat. Now, breathe. As you inhale, say to yourself, "Breathing in, I know that I am breathing in." As you exhale, say "Breathing out, I know that I am breathing out."

"Breathing in, I know that I am breathing in."

"Breathing out, I know that I am breathing out."

"Breathing in, I know that I am breathing in."

"Breathing out, I know that I am breathing out."

This technique is commonly written about in Buddhist meditation books, and the best one I have ever seen was written by Vietnamese Buddhist monk Thich Nhat Hanh. His book, *Peace is Every Step,* is the most powerful, enlightening book I have ever read because it taught me *how* to slow down and live. It is the best book on mindfulness I have ever seen.

Which brings us to the breathing in and breathing out exercise. Say the words as you breathe, and once you get used to it, you can replace the longer sentence with the words "in" as you inhale and "out" as you exhale. How simple. How wonderful. How liberating.

"We can smile, breathe, walk and eat our meals in a way that allows us to be in touch with the abundance of happiness that is available," he wrote. "We are very good at preparing to live, but not very good at living. We know how to sacrifice ten years for a diploma, and we are willing to work very hard to get a job, a car, a house, and so on. But we have difficulty remembering that we are alive in the present moment, the only moment there is for us to be alive. Every breath we take, every step we make, can be filled with peace, joy, and serenity. We only need to be awake, alive in the present moment."

This breathing exercise slows you down, and gets you to focus on the most necessary act of living: breathing. By doing this, breathing becomes a peaceful act.

EXERCISE: One Thing at a Time

Your assignment: Can you spend a day doing one thing at a time? Talk about a challenge. But try to spend a day without multi-tasking. If you are on the phone, be on the phone. If you are at dinner, be at dinner. If you are driving, drive. Just for a day, see if you can stop multi-tasking and start living.

1. Do you have a problem with multi-tasking? When are you most prone to be doing two or three things at once?

2. Has this problem gotten worse for you over time? Why?

3. What is going to be your biggest challenge to doing one thing at a time?

Okay, so do it. I dare you. One day. One thing at a time. If the thought is daunting, you've got to wonder why. Life has gotten so out of control for most of us that the thought of slowing down – truly slowing down – is unsettling. But, master this and you've got a tool that will replace the chaos in your life with a true calm.

EXERCISE: Eat Less. Enjoy it More.

I once attended Frannie Gerthoffer's lecture on mindful eating at the Hilton Head Health Institute. Okay, the story is this: I was brought in to speak there, and it's not just a health institute. It's a high-end weight-loss retreat where I got to stay and eat and work out for a full week. I loved it.

So, you can imagine my thrill when, a few days into the strict diet program, Frannie handed all of us a single milk chocolate Hershey's Kiss.

"Not yet!" she ordered as she walked us through the exercise.

First, she wanted us to unwrap the chocolate and look at it.

Then, smell it.

She told us to bring the Kiss to our lips, close our eyes and put the whole thing in our mouths.

Finally, she allowed us to bite down on it.

"Hold it!" she said. "Savor it!"

Oh, how I savored that taste.

"Okay, bite and hold again."

It was the most delicious chocolate I had ever tasted.

"After two tastes," she informed us, "You have experienced most of the taste sensation you are going to get."

That is a fact. It is science. Most of us can't wait to get to the second, third, and fourth piece of chocolate. We devour all of it without truly tasting or experiencing any of it. We aren't eating mindfully – we are just eating. We eat too much, and enjoy it too little.

So…

1. Go buy yourself a piece of chocolate.

2. Look at it. Smell it. Bite it and hold. Bite it and hold. Taste it.

Once you have seen how this works, try to be more mindful during your meals. Sit down at the dinner table. No television, no cell phone, and no reading. Don't even talk. Just savor every single bite and see what you've been missing.

EXERCISE: Go Outside and Take a Look Around.

Now move outdoors and savor what you see. Go for a walk and soak in the nature. Feel how good your body feels as you exercise. Feel the sun and the wind and soak it all in. Enjoy the trees and the birds and the color of the grass and the sky. Really *see* what you are experiencing and experience it with all your senses.

Finally, Live NOW, Not Later

Life is fragile and filled with uncertainty. You can waste so much time and energy worrying about things that will never happen. You can plan for every possibility, but life rarely unfolds according to plan. You can stress, distract, obsess and forget yourself through life, or you can live it.

We all have problems to worry about, but the past is gone and the future hasn't or might not happen. The only thing that is real is this very moment. Fill it with life and light.

PERSPECTIVE

Mindfulness is the aware, balanced
acceptance of the present experience.
It isn't more complicated than that.
It is opening to or receiving the present
moment, pleasant or unpleasant, just as
it is,
without either clinging to it or rejecting
it.
– Author Sylvia Boorstein

"Do not speak- unless it
improves on silence."
– Author Unknown

Let your love flow outward through the universe,
To its height, its depth, its broad extent,
A limitless love, without hatred or enmity.
Then as you stand or walk,
Sit or lie down,
As long as you are awake,
Strive for this with a one-pointed mind;
Your life will bring heaven to earth.
– Sutta Nipata (Buddhist Scripture)

The practice of mindfulness begins in the small, remote cave of your unconscious mind and blossoms with the sunlight of your conscious life, reaching far beyond the people and places you can see.
– Earon Davis, Teacher and Healer

"Life is not lost by dying; life is lost minute by minute, day by dragging day, in all the small uncaring ways."
– Author Stephen Vincent Benet

"The range of what we think and do is limited by what we fail to notice. And because we fail to notice that we fail to notice there is nothing we can do to change until we notice how failing to notice shapes our thoughts and deeds."
– R.D. Laing, Scottish Psychiatrist

Don't Force the Universe. Listen to it.

My favorite server at my favorite beach restaurant sighed at lunch today and said, "I need to do something different with my life, but I don't know what it is."

Yesterday, the exasperation came from a reader who e-mailed, "I'm still trying to find my passion – envious that you have found yours!"

I am asked the "What should I do now?" question all the time. I always say, "Put it out there and the universe will send you a signal."

My life's most pivotal changes occurred because I listened when somebody made a remark that could have easily been lost in passing. For example, in 1991, my friend suggested I rehab from knee surgery by training for Ride the Rockies, the classic Colorado bike challenge sponsored by The Denver Post. I did that bike trip and have taken a cycling vacation almost every year since. I cycle almost every day. It is my sanity and my salvation.

In 1998, as I struggled with my duties as a manager, I went looking for a book that would teach me how to succeed as a strong woman in a harsh work environment. When I couldn't find what I was looking for, a friend said, "Well, you're a journalist. Why don't you write that book?" That led to my first best-seller, *Hard Won Wisdom*. As I endured endless rejections and waited for that book to finally find its publisher, another friend threw out a suggestion. "Hey, you ought to be a professional speaker," she said. It had *never* occurred to me that I could have a career standing up in front of people and talking. That was the most significant and rewarding prompt that the universe ever gave me.

Those three remarks led me to my three strongest passions today: speaking, writing books and cycling. Although my friends made the suggestions, I had to be open to them. I had to follow through with action. The cycling in the Rocky Mountains took endless and exhausting hours of hard training. My life as an author began with endless obstacles that seemed insurmountable. My work as a speaker began by me doing things like driving six hours to Miami for an unpaid event where only 19 people showed up.

Even when I have been on my path, there have been countless opportunities for detours. Several years ago, I was courted for a job that came with a *really* fat weekly paycheck, great benefits, good vacation and a secure future. It didn't feel right for me, and I continued on my more uncertain route of self-employment as — gasp! — a motivational speaker. I had no idea that my route would ultimately prove much more stable and lucrative. I kept growing my business, and two years after I turned down that job, all the senior managers at that company were booted out. Some sought career advice from me.

It's important to know what you love and be mindful of the subjects or activities that are so exciting to you that you get completely lost in them. You'll often find the roots of passion there. But, also, listen up. Hear what others suggest and dare to take the steps to check things out. Try new things, but don't force the universe. You won't find great success by forcing yourself to love something that you don't even like.

And, if you are confused about what to do next, take heart. So are millions and millions of other people. The answers are out there. You just have to hear them — then act.

Ten Steps Out of Tough Times and Into Life Transition

If you're feeling worn out and frustrated by all of this talk of re-inventing yourself, have faith. It isn't going to kill you.

So much of the re-invention process comes down to making the decision to take charge of your life, then positioning yourself to actually do it.

1. Chill, Baby. You're on track now to do good things. Change is unsettling, but you are taking charge of your life. Celebrate.

2. Get dressed in the morning. Look good. Feel good so you can deliver.

3. Exercise. Do you stop exercising because you get depressed or do you get depressed because you stopped exercising? Do whatever you need to do in order to keep your depression at bay. Take your meds. Pray. Take care of yourself so you are able to deliver at your greatest level of performance.

4. Take charge of your brain. If you put negative in, you get negative out. Put positive in, get positive out. You have tremendous power to control what you are thinking and, when you start hearing the negative tapes, just give yourself a verbal "Stop" cue with your self-talk. Deliberately replace your negative thoughts with something positive. It's easier if you have a list of five positive things to go to for those low

moments. For example, "I've been so successful in the past. I'm smart enough to get through this."

5. Know that tough times will not last forever. As much as it feels like you are sinking into a bottomless pit of quicksand, you aren't. Don't let yourself slide into the mentality that says you may never change, win or find happiness. All that does is make you struggle more.

6. Remember who you are and who you are not. I see a lot of people who experience rejection and then process it as failure. They forget how talented and viable they are, so it becomes harder to project themselves as desirable. That poises them for more rejection. You have not lost your talent. And your setbacks have not erased your successes. They are just obstacles. You have succeeded in the past and you will succeed in the future.

7. Choose your friends carefully. If you surround yourself with hopeless people, you'll lose hope. This can be hard if most of your friends are former co-workers who were also laid off. And, that can be even worse if you are competing for the same jobs against your friends. You'll constantly wonder why someone got an interview or job that you didn't. Don't write those friends off, but focus on people who will propel your success.

8. Listen. What are you supposed to do with your life? The universe will send you many prompts. Great turning points often present themselves in passing. Know your weekly goals and achieve them by setting daily tasks. Then, DO THEM. Do something every day to move you closer to your goal.

The most important thing is to have faith. Things will work out. I am not being flip. I am not shrugging off your pain or uncertainty. Things do have a way of working out. I don't want to minimize anybody's suffering or delude myself into thinking that hope conquers all, but the truth is that there are very few of you who will wind up eating out of garbage cans. There's so much you can't control, so give it to the wind.

Get Out of Your Own Way

Look around you. I can pretty much guarantee that nine out of ten people you see have walloped themselves with a dose of negative self-talk today. Most of their negative thoughts started within an hour of waking up. They've fixated on their weight, their clothes, their blemishes, the jobs they are doing at work or at home, the kinds of parents they are, the job they've done with their finances. Their self-rejection goes on and on.

Is it any wonder that just about everybody has low self-esteem? This is the disease of our generation. We wallow in our imperfections until we drag ourselves down, and we feel even worse. We are meaner to ourselves than we are to total strangers and people we don't like. How do you think that affects what we do? It isn't going to make us great at achieving our goals.

If you think you are a loser, you start to act like a loser. If you think you look terrible, you start to look terrible. If you think you're dumb, you'll do dumb things.

I said earlier that I get a million bucks worth of free therapy every time I write a book. I learned that early on when I wrote *Hard Won Wisdom* and asked all of those accomplished leaders and trailblazers about their self-esteem. Almost every one of them admitted they had self-esteem issues that made them feel bad – but that they had made peace with their imperfections and went out into the world to do the best they could.

Their honesty gave me the power to hit the mute switch on the negative voice that used to operate in my head. For me, that was like hitting the emotional lottery. After all, if people I admired so much had the same self-esteem issues I had, the negativity *had* to be manufactured. When I stand in front of a room filled with gorgeous people and start talking about this, the room goes silent. When I bring it up at lunch with senior executives, they go silent as well. We assume certain people have got it all together. Guess what? They don't. That's because it truly is a universal problem. When I ask what bothers them most, the answer usually has something to do with how they look. Even the thinnest people say their weight bothers them; either they think they are too skinny or they think they are too fat. Can you imagine what the people on this earth would look like if we all looked as bad as we think we look? Pretty beastly.

Faye Wattleton, known for being savvy and brilliant and strategic leader of Planned Parenthood through some of its most tumultuous times, was also named to *People's* list of the 100 most beautiful people in the world. Despite all of that, she copped to "a profound sense of inadequacy." I will never forget her saying that. How could she have a self-esteem issue, especially since she had the esteem of so many people? Let me tell you: Almost every superstar has issues.

I was doing a keynote for Kraft last year and shouted out to its executive vice president for human resources. I said, "Karen, have you said anything negative to yourself today?" She didn't miss a beat. "My hair is flat and my pants are too short." She cracked up the audience. It wasn't even 10 a.m. and she'd already flogged herself, just like everybody else in the room.

If you could hear the negative thoughts that people around you have voiced in the last 24 hours, you would be floored. Most of what they say isn't true or doesn't matter. Or, if it is true and does matter, it isn't worthy of the nonstop barrage that they are inflicting on themselves.

If you are overweight, well, so what? Aside from the health concerns, you can be justifiably mad that you don't look your best. But, how many times do you need to bring it up? Once a week? Once a day? Twice a day? Look, I have had a weight issue all my life. I know how that works. You wake up and think you are fat. Then you tell yourself you are fat when you go to the closet to figure out what you are going to wear. And again when you are getting ready. And when you walk into the office and when you order at lunch and… it doesn't stop.

You feel lousy about yourself, which makes you nervous, which makes you eat. And you eat so much that you get fatter and that makes you say even nastier things about yourself, which makes you nervous and makes you eat and, finally, you get fed up and go on a diet. You lose some weight and feel great, but then you start eating again and then you gain the weight back and wake up feeling way worse, because not only are you overweight, you have the added embarrassment of having lost and regained weight. So, you eat and…

Stop it! Just cut it out. Make peace with what you look like today because you can't change everything in an instant. Why sacrifice this beautiful day to feeling inadequate? Why pull yourself down?

Eleanor Roosevelt said the classic line, "Nobody can make you feel inferior without your consent." She was controversial, bold, and always a target of critics, yet she kept on moving forward and made history.

Movie legend Sophia Loren once said, "Sex appeal is fifty percent what you've got and fifty percent what people think you've got." I would add that it isn't limited to just sex appeal – it's appeal in general. If other people think you've got it going on, you've got it going on. You attract what you project. If you project your best self, you'll attract your greatest possibility. If you project a weakened version of yourself, you will attract diluted opportunities, professionally *and* in your relationships.

You can spend your days loving or loathing yourself. Which is going to give you a better outcome? How do you start on a course to appreciating who you are? Well, do your homework.

Even when you are feeling your worst, you can give yourself a personal reality check that will remind you that you are not a total loser.

EXERCISE: Taking Stock

Spend some time thinking about the messages you have been playing in your head for the last week. Write down what you have been saying about the following topics:

How you look:

Your physical condition:

Your mental state:

How smart you are:

Your ability to fit in socially:

Your value to the world:

What others think of you:

How strong you are as an individual:

Your common sense:

Okay, now where do you think you got the negative tapes in your head? Take a minute to write down what the key players in your life did to build you up – or tear you down. What did your mother do? Your father? Brothers and sisters? Friends? Schoolmates? Bosses? Neighbors? Others?

Write down the ten key people who had the greatest impact on your self-esteem and some of the messages they gave you, good and bad:

1.

2.

3.

4.

5.

6.

7.

8.

9.

I tend not to believe it when people tell me they have great self-esteem. Because I've seen that some of the most revered people in America have self-esteem issues, I now know how to put negativity in its place. With all of that insider perspective, I have good self esteem – but I do have my moments. But I also know to shut down that inner dialogue – and fast. That brings me right back up.

The exercises in this chapter are designed to give you that very skill. In order to know how to shut down the negative voice, you need to first hear it in all of its power. That takes real focus and introspection because you may be aware that you say negative things about one aspect of your life, but not about another. You can't fix the problem until you take the time to figure out what you are saying, how often you are saying it and how it is coloring your overall feelings about yourself.

As you do the exercises in this chapter, remind yourself:

1. You can feel good about yourself, or bad. Your choice. You are now taking the steps to make yourself feel good.

2. You have great control over your inner negativity, and you are now going to take charge of it.

3. By focusing on your positive traits and putting your imperfections in perspective, you can live a happier and more productive life.

4. It's all up to you.

EXERCISE: Fifteen Minute Reality Check

Get ready to put your brain on autopilot and write as fast as you can. Your assignment is to write a sentence stating something you like about yourself. Do it in positive terms – not negative. For example, "I'm always on time" uses positive language. "I'm never late" uses negative. You've got fifteen minutes to come up with as many positive statements as possible. It doesn't matter how big or small. Just keep them coming.

For example: I have great eyes. My hair looks great. I have the best shoe collection on Earth. I'm a strong person. My mother loves me. I'm a good friend. I'm a great gardener. I'm a good idea person. I'm a great cook…

Just go as far as you possibly can with this and see how much you really have going for you.

When you start to feel bad about yourself, go back to your list. You have much to offer – do you realize your worth or choose to minimize yourself?

Okay, now it is serious list time. Tune out the negativity and spend some time taking inventory about what you really have to offer. Start by listing ten characteristics other people like about you.

Things Others Like About Me
1.
2.
3.
4.
5.
6.
7.
8.
9.
10.

Things I Like About Myself
1.
2.
3.
4.
5.
6.
7.
8.
9.
10.

What I Am Proud of
1.
2.
3.
4.
5.
6.
7.
8.
9.
10.

For this next exercise, take stock of your accomplishments – but don't limit it to things that would impress others. Sure, count career accomplishments and add in your beautiful kids. But count things like having the courage to dump a bad husband or learning to Hula-Hoop or being a good friend or cutting your long hair. Take time to take stock of the things that have made you the person you are.

50 Things I Have Done Right in Life
1.
2.
3.
4.
5.
6.
7.
8.
9.
10.
11.
12.

50 Things I Have Done Right in Life
13.
14.
15.
16.
17.
18.
19.
20.
21.
22.
23.
24.
25.
26.
27.
28.
29.
30.
31.
32.
33.
34.
35.
36.
37.
38.
39.
40.

50 Things I Have Done Right in Life
41.
42.
43.
44.
45.
46.
47.
48.
49.
50.

Ten Things That Make Me Happy
1.
2.
3.
4.
5.
6.
7.
8.
9.
10.

My Ten Biggest Achievements
1.
2.
3.
4.
5.
6.
7.
8.
9.
10.

Get a Grip

Three weeks ago, my friend Rene and her husband began to split up, I think. First, we heard there was going to be a divorce. Then came a horrible session in couples therapy where her husband berated her for her spending habits and then, when she pushed him to reveal whether he had somebody else, he literally snarled, "There's always somebody else."

He's still in the home, but he is cold and distant and cruel and making it clear he wants out and can't stand her.

He's told her she is worthless, stupid, unattractive, undesirable, unworthy, and the list goes on. And since he's got her in a vulnerable moment, she has accepted all that negativity and processed it so she feels worthless and stupid and all those other things.

But that isn't Rene. I know this woman. She's lovely and attractive and fun. I love her energy and her smile and her warmth and her insight. The only thing unworthy about her is her worthless ass of a husband. Sorry, but I'm ticked off.

I'm ticked off because she has been trying so hard to figure out what she needs to do to win him back. I'm ticked off because she told me yesterday that she feels so humiliated. *She* feels humiliated? The one who should feel humiliated is the one who cheated and lied and then turned the blame on the wife he deceived and betrayed. I don't judge people who are unfaithful because I've watched my friends suffer on both sides of those relationships, and I realize the judgment will be between the people involved and the universe. What I do judge is cruelty, that someone can betray and deceive someone, then turn the blame on the victim and tell her that it is all her fault.

And what really makes me mad is that it works. My friend is humiliated.

This is not simply about a woman dealing with a cheating spouse. It is a story about those of us whose self-esteem is not strong enough to hold them up when others hold them down. Rene doesn't have the self-esteem to look that jackass in the eyes and say, "Get out of this house. I will not be talked to like that. You will not turn the blame on me."

The same thing happens when a teenager verbally assaults you as a parent: The parent either stops it or raises a bully. I sadly admit that, when I was in high school, the day came when I called my mother the b-word. Once. I mean it. Once. She told me she wasn't going to take it and, in fact, she was going to take my stereo from me – which she did, until I left for college six months later.

There are mean or catty people at work, in our neighborhoods, at the PTA, in our churches, gyms and social groups. Sometimes, we become the target of *their* insecurities in a way that makes us question our own value. I have always noticed that the biggest bullies and the most arrogant people among us are truly insecure people who choose to overpower others in order to make themselves seem important. Their victims rarely step out of the situation to look at what is really happening; instead, they accept the negativity that is heaped on them.

I've often told the story of the boss I had who told me I would never be any more than a newspaper reporter. That story is relevant here because it took me two years to stop trying so hard to win his favor and respect. Instead of looking at him and realizing that he was a real jerk, I tried to please him by working even harder and doing everything I could to get him to notice how worthy I was. He never did, of course, but I finally started looking at how he was treating others. Then I realized that I wasn't the problem. He was.

So when someone has treated you poorly and put you down, you can wait years for the revelation that the problem is the other person's – not yours – or you can do this next exercise to help you change your point of view. ***Use this exercise when somebody gets in your way and makes you feel bad about yourself. And remember the Eleanor Roosevelt quote: "Nobody can make you feel inferior without your consent." This exercise is for those times when you catch yourself giving your consent.***

1. Describe the situation where the other person has made you feel inadequate.

2. List the negative things this person has said to you.

3. Why have you allowed this person to say these things?

4. What is it that makes this person's opinion so much more important than your own?

5. Are you strong enough to take a barrage of negativity and know your true internal worth regardless of what the other person thinks?

6. Do you have a history of letting others influence how you feel about yourself? Why do you allow that?

7. Have you heard this person put down other people? Why do you think he or she does that?

8. If you could freely talk back to this person without fear of retribution, what would you say? How would you say it? Then what would you do?

9. What would it take to shut this person up?

10. What is the risk involved in talking back? What could you do to minimize the damage?

11. Why are you feeling bad, rather than taking your power and setting boundaries so you will be treated well?

12. What are you going to do to change that?

Volunteer. Do Good Things.

One of the best ways to climb out of negativity quicksand is to do something to help other people. But you don't have to go spend a day with a hammer and a saw from Habitat for Humanity in order to get the kind of emotional high you get from volunteering. You can get high by being a good person every day.

Tip well. Mentor others. Be there for friends. Help someone carry something heavy. Clean out your closet and give the good stuff to the needy. Be nice. Volunteering your time and love is so life-affirming that it's funny that others are so thankful for our assistance when they are actually helping *us*. Whenever you are feeling down on yourself, reach out and help someone else.

Instead of focusing on the worst in yourself, do something that helps you see the best in yourself. Be good, be kind, be giving, and all the heavy stuff seems a little lighter.

PERSPECTIVE

"It's not who you are that holds you back, it's who you think you're not."
– Author Unknown

"If you really put a small value upon yourself, rest assured that the world will not raise your price."
– Author Unknown

"It is not the mountain we conquer but ourselves."
– Edmund Hillary

"Without a humble but reasonable confidence in your own powers you cannot be successful or happy."
– Norman Vincent Peale
"When the grass looks greener on the other side of the fence, it may be that they take better care of it there."
– Cecil Selig

"You have brains in your head.
You have feet in your shoes.
You can steer yourself in any direction
you choose.
You're on your own.
And you know what you know.
You are the guy who'll decide where to
go."
– Dr. Seuss

"We are all such a waste of our potential, like three-way lamps using one-way bulbs" – Mignon McLaughlin, The Neurotic's Notebook, 1960

It's me who is my enemy
Me who beats me up
Me who makes the monsters
Me who strips my confidence.
– Paula Cole, "Me," This Fire

"The way you treat yourself sets
the standard for others."
– Sonya Friedman

Trust Your Instincts

It was five minutes from darkness and I was literally lost in the Gulf of Mexico in my kayak. The fog was so thick that I could only see about forty feet in any direction. The water was very deep, and my kayak was taking on water. I wondered if I was going to die.

I was kayaking in the TenThousand Islands part of Everglades National Park with a group I'd discovered online. This is the part of the Everglades that is open water and glorious – not the part filled with snakes and alligators. But it is huge, and very, very easy to get lost in.

I went with a guide who I'll call Dakota Dave, who I'd found online on Meetup.com. With us were his assistant and three guys. I took my own kayak, not knowing that it a) was far inferior to the sleek, fast, touring kayaks the others had and b) had a bad leak.

We met at the Everglades City ranger station at 8 a.m. The weather was already worse than anything I'd ever gone kayaking in: Thick fog and heavy current. If I'd seen those conditions back at home, I would never have launched. But the group acted like it was no big deal, so I pretended to be nonplussed.

When we checked in, we were told that Rabbit Key already had eight campers on it and we'd have to paddle an extra five miles to Pavilion Key if we were going to camp.

That meant hours of extra kayaking, but I didn't say anything. I should note here that I am in fairly good shape and am no sissy.

I should also note that this story may involve a kayak and a kayaker, but it is every one of us. It is about trusting our instincts and using our power. It's about going against the grain when we know we are right and others are waiting for someone to take the lead.

So, while you read this, ask yourself what you would have done if you were in my situation.

From the minute we launched our boats, I could not keep up. When the others would stop to wait for me, I'd paddle hard to catch up and, once I did, they were ready to go again. I quickly became exhausted and dehydrated, but I pushed on. Within a few hours, the fog became so thick that we would go for a very, very long time without seeing land. Our guide was using the old system of navigation – compass and map – and kept pointing in the direction the group was to go. Because my boat was slower and had that leak, I was always behind everyone and off to the side because of drifting. From that vantage point I could see something very disturbing: We were going in circles.

We stopped for lunch on what he said was Jack Daniels Key. It wasn't Jack Daniels Key. Thirty minutes after lunch, Dakota Dave pointed to an island and said, "Oh, *that's* Jack Daniels Key." For the next several hours, we saw only an occasional spit of land. By mid-afternoon, we landed on what he said was Rabbit Key – the island we'd initially hoped to camp on, but couldn't because the rangers limit the number of campers to prevent environmental damage. We had another five miles to go, but I had no more energy.

"I'm staying here," I told Dakota Dave.

I'd had enough. My boat was literally fighting me. Combined with the current, wind and fog, I was absolutely depleted. I'd tried so hard not to fall behind. Like I said, I am in shape. I am strong. But, I wondered if they saw my desire to stop paddling as a sign that the oldest person was the weakest link. I was in my late 40s. Most of them were in their 20s and 30s.

"The rangers will find you and make you leave," Dave said.

"I'll ask them for a ride."

"You can't stay here."

"Yes, I can. I am exhausted."

"You have to stay with the group." Dave said.

I thought to myself, *What are you going to do? Club me in the head?*

"Look," he said. "We can tow you if it gets to be too much. Really, it won't be long."

Okay, what would you have done?

The only reason I continued on from that point was the camping area on the beach was so small that I was concerned it would be totally covered when the tide came in.

Soon, we were paddling again. It wasn't long before we saw a big, beautiful island in our view and he proclaimed, "We're here!"

I couldn't believe it. In fact, I was elated. I'd done it!

But, as we circled around to the front of the island, he shook his head.

"This is Rabbit Key, not Pavilion."

I thought we'd already been to Rabbit Key.

"We have to go on," he said.

It was getting too late to go another five miles, but I said nothing. We headed out, and we'd paddled about two miles when he scratched his head and said we had to turn around *again* because he decided the island we'd really left behind was Pavilion Key – our destination.

We headed back. We were two minutes from landing on that pristine beach when he shook his head and said, "Sorry, but this isn't Pavilion. It's Rabbit." Dakota Dave turned us back around. Again. Would you believe we paddled for another fifteen minutes when he stopped us *again* and said, "No, that *was* Pavilion. We need to turn around."

So, we turned around again. Back and forth, back and forth, back and forth – I was angry but also so relieved we were heading back to that beautiful island where I could finally put my paddle down and drink some water.

Five minutes later, he scratched his head again and led us up and down the full length of the island, then around the back, then back out front.

"No, he said. "This is Rabbit Key. We have to keep going. We have 90 minutes of daylight. We have to paddle *now.*"

The panic in his voice was evident. The fog was so thick that we could barely see anything. Everyone was exhausted.

"Let's just stay here on Rabbit Key," I said.

"We can't," he said. "The rangers will make us leave in the middle of the night."

First of all, the likelihood of the rangers coming out to check on us in that weather was pretty small. But, the likelihood of them kicking us off an island like that and sending us out in dangerous weather like that was zero.

"They aren't going to do that." I said.

"Yes they will. We need to paddle. *Now.*"

"I think we should stay here. There is plenty of room and it is too dangerous to go out."

"We have time. We have to leave now. You are slowing this down and we don't have time to waste."

Okay, I ask you. What would you have done? Seriously. I know it is easier to decide what you would have done when you aren't out in the middle of the lonely Gulf and faced with the decision, but would you have left the others behind and paddled to that island?

My body tensed up. I *knew* following him was a huge mistake. I also knew that I was carrying the group's dinner in my kayak. If I turned in and paddled to shore, they'd *have* to follow. By the time we hit ground so they got the food, it would probably be too late for them to go back out.

My mind raced. *"I should stay. Stay, Fawn! But, what about the other people who will come to camp on the island? They might be rednecks. They could hurt me. I won't know how to get back to the ranger's station. I have no idea where I am. We are miles and miles away from civilization. But, this guide doesn't know what he's doing!"*

My gut knew that following him was a mistake. "Don't follow him! You are exhausted! You are dehydrated! Stay behind..."

I looked at one of the burly guys who was paddling near me and when we made eye contact, he shrugged. I now realize that his shrug was a sign that he didn't know what to do. He was waiting for *me* to take charge. He didn't want to make a fuss because he'd seem weak. I didn't realize it.

I worried that my resistance made me sound like a complainer and a wimp. Why was I worried what those people were thinking?

I had the courage to speak up and talk back, yet I did not act.

What holds us back?

Do you realize how often we all do that? We shut down our gut instincts because we worry that our resistance will make us unpopular.

My decision to go with the others came down to three things:

1. I had no clue where I was. Even my lousy guide was better than no guide. I had no idea how to get back to civilization.

2. If I stayed on Rabbit Key, I would either be camping by myself or with a) nice people, b) rednecks, c) killers, or d) redneck killers.

None of the other kayakers in my group backed me up. Was I imagining the gravity of the situation? My gut knew it was a mistake, but we headed out again in search of Pavilion Key.

The conditions worsened as we paddled. The guide kept calling out to the assistant, asking the time and trying to determine where in the world we were with a method where he would calculate time against distance traveled and apply it to the map. Two things made this effort futile: He had no idea where we were on the map to begin with, and he could not calculate distance traveled in relation to time since the conditions were getting worse by the minute, making us go slower and slower.

His voice grew more panicked. He clipped the front of my rudderless boat to his boat so the current wouldn't push me so far away from the rest of the group.

I thought of a recent news story about three men whose boat capsized after a big wave flipped them over in the Gulf. Two men – both NFL football players – died. Their friend survived. I thought about them and how my kayak was taking on so much water.

I prayed. I thought about my family. My pets. I thought about how my mother had suffered so much with illnesses for 18 years of her life. "God," I prayed. "If this is the way you plan to take me out, I am okay with it. Because this sure beats suffering like my mom has. But if this isn't what you have in mind, you need to do something now." Just then, an island appeared in the mist. It was not Pavilion key. Our guide had no idea where we were. But, we had reached land. Because I was so exhausted, I collapsed in my tent. I soon realized I was very dehydrated, but didn't have the energy to get up, walk 20 feet to my boat, and get myself a gallon of water. I called out to the assistant guide and asked if she could bring me a jug of water from my kayak. She did, and I immediately drank two-thirds of that gallon jug.

Around the campfire, our guide patted himself on the back for getting us to safety. He should have been flogged for putting us in danger. At some point, he admitted he had no idea where we were. I asked him why he didn't have a GPS with him.

"I use a compass. A GPS can break," he said.

"That's when you use the compass," I shot back.

After dinner, one of the guys noticed he had faint cellular reception on his phone. I checked mine and I was able to dial out and call home. Once my loved ones knew that I was out there with that goofball, I felt safer. They knew to take action if I didn't call within 24 hours.

There were so many pivotal moments where I had to decide whether to do what I knew in my gut was right, or go along with someone who had much more experience and knowledge, who was in a position of authority.

It is all about having the self-confidence to stand up, be firm and act when you are the lone voice. Do you have the courage to defy your leader, leave the group, and travel unprotected when you know in your gut that you are right and the others are wrong? This is about self-navigation – not kayaking. Can you find your greatness without fully embracing your power? And isn't that an ongoing challenge?

It is. I wrote a book called *Mustang Sallies*, about having the courage to be a mustang and knowing when to leave the herd behind. I'm pretty adept at doing that in business situations, but when it came to a situation that put my life in danger, I had to learn a new lesson.

People are constantly following incompetent bosses, significant others, friends, politicians, community leaders, neighbors, and others. Why? Because those inept people seem like they know something just because they act like they know it. We forget that we give them power and, too often, stop thinking or acting for ourselves because the leader out front is speaking with authority. We stand with the crowd, silent.

Can You Leave the Group?

Okay, let's say it was you in the kayak. What would you have done?

How likely are you to speak up in a situation where you know the group is headed in the wrong direction?

How likely are you to act on your concerns and go it alone?

How important is it for you to feel validated and accepted by the people around you?

Do you stand up for yourself? What does it take to get you to speak up?

Can you think of any situations in your life when it has seemed like the person in charge didn't know what the he or she was talking about? Did others follow? Did you? Describe the situation.

How do you feel when you go against the norm?

Are you someone who makes peace with the status quo or someone who tries to change it?

How do you let the opinions of others influence what you say or do?

Finally Taking My Power

Back to the Everglades and the kayak trip. The next morning started out extremely foggy, which meant I could be in for a repeat of Day One. Should I go back into the fog or wait on land? I finally decided to take charge of myself. While the others ate breakfast, I went into my tent and used my cell phone to call the ranger's station back in Everglades City.

Finally, I took full responsibility for myself. I told the ranger what had happened the day before, and that I had no idea where I was.

"I just wanted you to know I'm out here," I said. As if that helped. There is a reason the place is called the Ten Thousand Islands.

"The smartest thing you can do is stay put," he said. "We can track your cell phone signal."

I said I'd stay behind if it was still foggy at launch time. If the fog lifted, I would launch. But when they launched an hour later, the sun had burned off and we were blessed with the most glorious day of kayaking I'd ever experienced. There were islands *everywhere*, which was shocking. We had spent the previous day feeling completely lost in the middle of a vast, menacing sea, but we didn't know there was land all around us.

Sunlight danced on top of the water. It was warm and wonderful. But I still had a big problem: I couldn't keep up. When we stopped for lunch, I saw the marker to one of the two passes that led back to the start. Another paddler told me that he wanted to go back with me if I went back. I told Dakota Dave, who insisted that we stay with the group. But I was going back. My boat was completely exhausting me.

"Let me try your boat," he said. He took it out for a few minutes, then came back. "I don't know how you have made it this far in that boat."

I knew there was water inside the boat, but when we lifted it to drain it, I was stunned by the amount. Water dumped out for more than five minutes. Gallons and gallons – at least sixty or seventy pounds of it. That, along with my camping gear, made my kayak impossible to propel and control. Dakota Dave had me switch boats with the assistant guide, and suddenly I was free, up at the front of the group, enjoying the day. When we got to Picnic Key, we frolicked in the Gulf.

Dave promised that Day Three would be 2 ½ hours of easy paddling because the tide would sweep us right in once we got to the pass. We just had to launch by 8 a.m. to be there by 10 a.m. The wind was terrible, but it wasn't scary because the sun was out and we could see land at all times.

We got to the pass right on time, and there were three options: Go to the left, right or center. Dakota Dave chose to go to the right, but before he did, I said, "Um, don't you think we should go to the center where there is that channel marker?" He seemed annoyed. "I know what I'm doing here."

Apparently not. We paddled for hours in worsening tidal conditions:. Because the day was supposed to be short and easy, I opted to get in my leaky boat again. As the current worsened, it was harder to control than ever. Dave was getting more nervous with every stroke, as it was obvious we'd made the wrong turn, missed the tide and we were going to have to fight truly treacherous currents to get in.

"Do you know where we are?" Mike, another paddler, asked.

Dakota Dave said nothing.

"Do you know where we are?" Mike demanded, even louder.

Again, no response. Dave had no idea where we were or how to get us out of there. That was a big deal. There are only two cuts in and out of the place. We'd left the first one behind, but where was the second? If we'd passed that already, we were headed miles into nowhere.

In the distance, we heard a boat. Dave held his paddle straight up over his head, which is the distress signal, and he instructed us all to do the same. Thankfully, the boat came toward us. It was a ranger from the National Park Service.

It wasn't long before the ranger determined that our guide was operating an expedition without a license, scolded him and issued him a $500 ticket. He showed us the way out and we faced the most horrendous winds and current of the trip. We landed at Everglades City at about 4 p.m.

All I wanted was to be home with my family. And it has taken me four months to process what the experience meant to my life.

Dakota Dave was a nice guy but a terrible guide. I bet he would have a very different story than mine, but I can't help but wonder if he learned anything out there.

I sure did.

I'm not as strong as I thought, but I'm getting stronger.

The universe is a great teacher.

Peace Within

When I go to bed at night, I imagine earth from above. There are 6.8 billion people down here and every single one of us thinks that the world begins and ends right where we stand. We think our problems are huge, but usually, they aren't. Not when you look at what others face. I'm not an astronomer, but I get lost in images from space. They bring me peace. And, perspective, because sometimes I imagine what God sees. In my lifetime, I've spent too much time worrying about problems rather than seeing them for how small they are. What makes me think that my problems are so important? My place in the universe is so small.

It's humbling.

Here I am.

There's one of me.

In a country of 304 million people. On a planet of 6.8 billion people.

Our problems are not the worst problems in the world. The universe doesn't revolve around us. It feels like it, but, no. It doesn't.

There are hundreds of billions of stars in our galaxy and there are at least 50 billion galaxies in the universe. They say there are ten million billion planets. And I am just one person, taking up this tiny little space in one tiny little city in one tiny little country on one tiny little planet in one tiny little galaxy.

So, I think about this, and I feel peace.

I look back on the best moments in my life and realize that the greatest thrills I experienced cost nothing. They were moments of love and prayer and family and friendship. They were moments of nature and laughter and personal discovery or triumph. If I had to choose between $50 million or a life without the people I love or God or my pets or the nature around me, I would never choose the money. And health? You can't put a pricetag on that. Every healthy breath is worth $50 million.

You made it through last year. You'll make it through this one.

How?

Persevere.

Don't waste a single day of your life, because time is always precious. No one is on earth forever, and whether you are experiencing ease or adversity, you can enjoy what you have.

Count your blessings, then count them again. That'll keep you grounded.

When you feel worn out, remember to slow down and breathe deeply, grateful that you are safe and secure in who you are, sure that you can handle anything if you just take life a day at a time. You will get past any adversity. You are smart. Smart people survive.

No matter what.

When it seems like everything is going all wrong, it's hard to see that you're really all right.

But, you are.

The Ah-Hah! Moment is when you realize you already have a brain. You already have courage. You already have a heart. It's when you realize you already have all the answers within you.

Fawn's Nonfiction Books

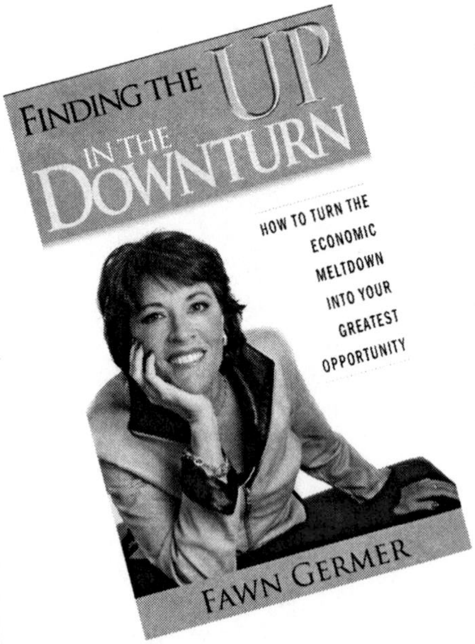

Best-selling author Fawn Germer has written five books which have become the cornerstones of her leadership and performance keynotes. These great books bring together the wisdom of America's most accomplished leaders and trailblazers.

Finding the UP in the Downturn

Spring, 2009
Newhouse Books

There is a Chinese proverb that says, "Fall down seven times, get up eight." Right now, as your co-workers, neighbors, friends and family members swallow their daily dose of bad news and see only bad times ahead, take a deep breath. While everyone else is giving in or giving up, your moment has arrived. Whether you want to gain ground in your corporate job, have recently been laid off, or are flirting with starting a business, a downturn can be the right time to charge ahead. Bestselling author Fawn Germer shows us how the one variable we can control – ourselves — is our most powerful weapon in the battle for prosperity and success. Germer documents that now is not the time to stop, but to accelerate.

The NEW Woman Rules

Fall, 2007
The Network of Executive Women

The most powerful women in American business today cleared their calendars for exhaustive interviews with best-selling author Fawn Germer. They shared their personal triumphs and defeats, and passed on what they learned the hard way. After completing more than fifty interviews, Fawn distilled a comprehensive list of more than 200 "how-to" rules for leadership and success that cannot be found anywhere else. The "new woman" *is* ruling, and this book shows how. Among her interview subjects are CEOs from Kraft, eBay, PepsiCo, Reynolds America, Sweetbay, Pathmark, Sara Lee and more. Joining them are the most senior women executives from Walmart, Procter and Gamble, General Mills, Campbell's Soup, Chevron, Johnson and Johnson and others.

Mustang Sallies

Fall, 2004
Penguin / Perigee Books

"Germer's advice is specific and illuminating. If you've ever felt judged and isolated at work for being who you are, Germer's book offers support, encouragement and strategies for coming through with your self and your goals intact." — *Publisher's Weekly*

Mustangs were the original wild horses of the West: tough, agile, quick to learn-and unwilling to run with the herd. And, like the daring woman in the famous song, today's Mustang Sallies question the rules, challenge the status quo, and dare to make a little noise. For this book, Fawn interviewed everyone from Hillary Clinton to Martina Navratilova to Susan Sarandon to Erin Brockovich and more than 75 others. The result is an engaging, provocative guide for women determined to charge ahead and succeed on their own terms.

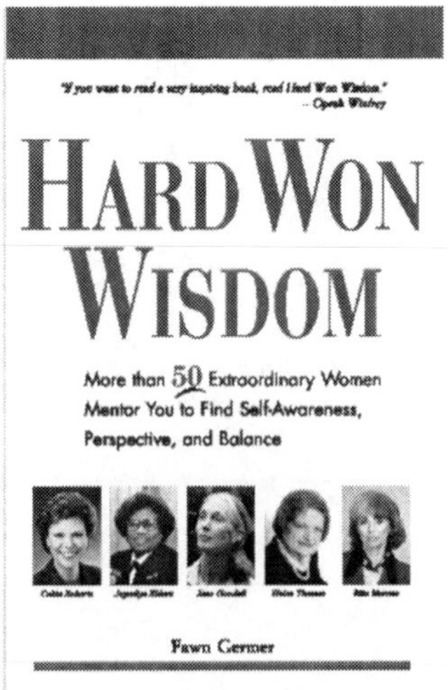

Hard Won Wisdom

Fall, 2001
Penguin / Perigee Books

"If you want to read a very inspiring book, read *Hard Won Wisdom.*"
— *Oprah Winfrey*

Hard Won Wisdom captured Oprah's fancy and launched Fawn onto the best-seller list. The book features inspiration and mentoring advice from Nobel Peace Prize winners, women presidents and prime ministers, Academy Award winners, Olympic Athletes and more. Fawn interviewed fifty icons, from Jane Goodall to Helen Thomas to Cokie Roberts and Rita Moreno. They share a perspective on self-awareness and balance that will dare you to leave your rut and redefine yourself in extraordinary terms. It hits hard at the self-esteem issues that hold so many women back, and offers a clear strategy to lift readers out of their anxiety and onto a success path.

Introduction to

Hard Won Wisdom

By Fawn Germer

By now, I've lost count of the number of times I have left work wondering if it was me who was crazy—or everybody else. Believe me, I have had enough of those days, weeks, months, and even years when I've felt worn out and wondered how I'd survive emotionally, much less professionally.

We all have. What's the deal? I read the same newspapers you do. Every day there is another headline telling us how far we've come. Why, here's a story about a woman, a CEO in a Fortune 500 company! And look at that one: *She* plays soccer. There's one running for president. That one's directing films, publishing books, commanding the space shuttle—not to mention the one who was in charge of foreign affairs . . .

Before I started connecting with this kind of woman in search of the hard-won wisdom from which the rest of us could benefit, I wondered whether we were even working on the same planet. They were leaping tall buildings in a single bound, and I was running head-on into the wall of office politics as a newspaper editor. I wondered why there were so many books telling us how to dress, how to talk, how to act and how to break through the glass ceiling—but *none* telling us how to survive it all emotionally.

Hopefully, with some of our generation's boldest women as our mentors, *Hard Won Wisdom* will fill that void. The idea for this book was to get the women who paved the road to show us how they did it, and let them mentor us from afar. They are joined by some of the nation's foremost experts in women's psychology, business and sociology who help synthesize the advice, inspiration and insight into a prescription for success. This book is the result of hundreds of interviews—done in person or by phone—with women leaders who have experienced the same obstacles and challenges that we encounter as we try to balance our professional and personal lives.

What surprised me most when I talked to these women was their willingness to speak so openly, sharing their own pain and triumph while relating what they have learned to our struggle today. What emerged was a concept of boldness that, once embraced, gives us permission to succeed, to fail, to try, to live. Their collective wisdom, which was certainly hard-won, is now a permanent resource that you and I can consult every time we need a little coaching or emotional boost.

These women give us validation, hope, and a game plan that will guide us through the minefield of competitive work environments that aren't always nice, fair or nurturing. They urge us to embrace chance, opportunity and the spirit by finding the right balance to support every personal challenge. And, they show us how to live a more fulfilling life.

What shocked me was how much I learned from women whose experiences are so removed from my own. I *never* imagined that a hockey player, dogsled racer, oceanographer or an anthropologist who focuses on primates would have advice that would apply to my world. But, they did. These women cut their paths in male-dominated fields, fighting the very same battles that many of us face. They have experienced as many tough days as the rest of us, and they've kept pushing.

These women didn't just "happen" upon greatness. They focused on it. They achieved what once seemed so impossible, not because they sought glory, but because they didn't have a choice. It burned inside of them. They latched on to what meant most to them and chased their passions. Their reward was the same sense of purpose that we all can experience by finding our own calling and doing what matters most to us.

So, we aren't the crazy ones. We are women who want to read and learn from others who have something to share. The women who share their wisdom here don't pretend to have every answer or to be any more worldly than the rest of us. They've had their share of battles, too, and hate that any of us still have to struggle. That's why they're talking now.

Imagine what we can do next, if only we listen.

Introduction to

Mustang Sallies

By Fawn Germer

SEVERAL years ago, one of my bosses sat me down in his office and told me, "You've gone as far as you're going to go. All you are now is all you are ever going to be-a reporter." I think of him as "The Tormentor,"- the very opposite of a mentor.

He hated my hard-charging ways and the issues I wanted to cover. I was a mustang, and I didn't know the rules of engagement. I could have avoided a lot of grief had I been coached by the women in this book. I'll never forget the day when he called me into his office, told me I would no longer cover women's issues, swore my lifelong dream of having a column would "never happen," and told me I wasn't going anywhere.

Despite the investigative reporting that had gotten me numerous state and national awards and four Pulitzer nominations, he told me I was to spend more than six weeks writing daily Christmas features, and after that, I'd cover the beat of his choosing. Obviously enjoying his power trip, he would not even deign to tell me what that beat would be.

Apparently, since he couldn't tame me, he'd just try to break my spirit. I felt demoralized, and my self-esteem plunged. My work performance suffered as I slacked off in protest. Finally realizing I was turning myself into a victim, I started working hard again. After two years, the metro editor promoted me into management.

I couldn't believe I'd gotten beyond my difficulties until I attended my initial afternoon news meeting with a dozen other editors, including The Tormentor. In that two years, he had moved way up the ladder and was now everyone's boss. "Fawn is here today because she's our new night assistant city editor," my metro editor announced. Right in front of everybody, The Tormentor declared, "She's just a reporter." I just stared, speechless, as I realized there would be no title and no raise — despite what was promised.

After the meeting, I went to my desk, picked up the telephone, and called the editor at another newspaper who had been trying to recruit me for several years. "If you want me," I told him, "make it happen now." He did.

It took me two days to write the previous six paragraphs.

Even though we move on and up, some old lessons are especially hard to learn, and the hurt feelings and anger don't go away just because we ultimately triumph. I was a hard-charging mustang and because of that, I paid a painful price. What I wouldn't have given for the coaching of Ann Richards, Claudia Kennedy, Erin Brockovich, Pat Heim, and the other mustangs I've talked to for the past year. I hope you won't have to pay like I did, which is why I wrote this book. I just want you to know that you are not crazy and you are not alone. Almost all of the bold, successful women I've interviewed for this book have had soul-challenging experiences like the rest of us and have learned to win in arenas where they were not appreciated or acknowledged.

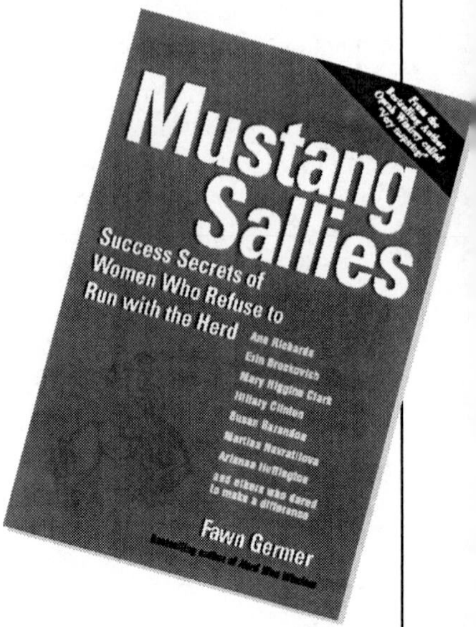

Every woman can be a mustang. We are everywhere, in every possible socioeconomic class, education level, and rank on the ladder. You may be in organized labor or in the corporate world, in politics or in the arts. I don't care if you work in a law firm or a grocery store, a Fortune 500 company or a Burger King. The mustang spirit lives.

Life is so sweet when you take your power and use it for yourself. If you feel stuck, unstick yourself. Don't listen to your tormentors, and don't torment yourself. You have the right to feel good about who you are, love what you do, and do it well. When you think you are trapped in a bad relationship, you aren't. When you feel sure no one else will want you, they will. If the job is dragging you way down, move on. If you are scared you can't get a job elsewhere, you can. Would I have ever left that job if "The Tormentor" hadn't been so cruel? I'd have missed out on the greatest adventure of my life: writing this. It's amazing. Every time you find yourself in a moment of self-definition, no matter how dark it is, you have the power to turn it into light. Be bold.

Introduction to

The NEW Woman Rules

By Fawn Germer

Midway into this book, I realized what the women leaders I'd interviewed had done. They'd handed me the secret code.

I knew I'd been shown something that no one else had seen, and I was overwhelmed by it, partly because of the power of the content, mostly because of the sincerity of the women. They climbed over so many obstacles to get to the top, and now they are reaching down to you – through me. There are more than fifty women in this book, all of whom have no spare time – none – but they cleared time for you because they don't like being alone at the top.

Success is not a finite commodity. There is enough for all of us. If they help you to succeed and you help the next women, our place in this world will grow. And grow. They know that. They know we can only embrace our possibility if we embrace each other.

Sometimes it seems like we are just crawling along. This year, women run thirteen of America's Fortune 500 companies. Last year, it was ten.

Wow, thirteen women at the very top, and there are only 140 million American women in the running.

It is easy to be cynical – or jubilant. Your choice. Not that long ago, women were banned from the Harvard Law School Library because we might distract men from their studies. We couldn't get credit in our own names. Employers fired us if we got pregnant, or didn't hire us because we *might* conceive. We were excluded from jury duty because, apparently, our opinion didn't count. There were male bosses who freely demanded sex from the women who worked for them – without consequence.

It wasn't so long ago that classified ads used to be split in half, with one set of jobs – the good ones – for men, and the rest for women. It was legal to pay men more because, well, just because.

Our history inspires me because our gains were the result of a brilliant, deliberate campaign for equality that began with the most crucial battle – the fight for the right to vote. Ninety years ago, we couldn't even vote! But, our foremothers knew that, if we could vote, we could make change. In the 1960s and 1970s, the Women's Liberation Movement and the National Organization for Women executed a brilliant strategy that made discrimination laws fall like dominos. Reading that history is so exciting and inspiring. The women who are now in their fifties, sixties and seventies fought those battles – for us. We have a legacy to protect – and create.

There are times when I get so discouraged, like when I see a Catalyst report that says only 6.7 percent of the top-paying positions in the Fortune 500 belong to women.

But then again, there are times like this moment when I see the potential that exists because of who we are as women. We are growing into our power – together. Learning from our mistakes and triumphs – together.

The first time I tried to get an interview with eBay CEO Meg Whitman, I got the same answer that I'd gotten from the other women CEOs on the Fortune 500 – a polite-but-firm no. The reason was the same, every time. The CEOs wanted to be viewed as CEOS – not as "women CEOs." It was as if the qualifier suggested "less than." But, I asked Whitman's spokesman if he would pass on a memo that I would write. He agreed, and I spent quite a bit of time composing my argument.

Some women know innately what it takes to break through in difficult environments. They know how to use their strength without being punished for it. They know how to fly above the politics and build teams that perform.

It doesn't come so naturally to all of us. That doesn't mean the rest of us are less able or deserving – it means we need a little guidance so we can get our chance to prove our mettle.

If the intuitive leaders don't share what they know instinctively, they will always be viewed as "women CEOs" because they will be the only ones up there. If they share their wisdom and enlighten the rest of us, they won't be so rare.

Whitman wound up giving me an incredible interview. I loved her. The other "women CEOs" didn't come around in that book, and I couldn't figure out why they wouldn't share their mentoring wisdom. Fortunately, a new lineup of great women is in power, and they not only agreed to participate this time – many said it was their duty.

You are their legacy. What you do with what they will teach you here will play out over years and even decades. Just don't do it alone. Remember the women coming up behind you, and help them along. The more success you create for others, the more you will succeed for yourself.

When I went through the interviews in this book and distilled "the rules," I realized that, collectively, their words created a legacy that could have a life-altering impact on the careers of thousands of women leaders. Will this book create one more Fortune 500 CEO? A book won't do that. But a movement to continue to share and reveal and help and mentor will create one, then two, then a dozen, then a hundred.

It's our moment. Our turn. Our rules.

If one woman gets over the wall, then brings two more, who each bring two more… You get the point. The world is ours.

Great Leaders Count On Fawn Germer

"Fawn hits us squarely in the eyes. She urges us to leave behind any 'woe is me' thinking, get up, dust ourselves off and put ourselves in a position to win."
Mike Salzberg, *President, Campbell Sales Company, the $3.2 billion arm of the Campbell's Soup Company.*

"If you take nothing else away from your encounter with Fawn Germer, you will learn that striving to outdo yourself will make almost anything possible. Fawn urges people to take risks, push themselves to their limits and believe in themselves – and have fun while doing so! I believe her new book will inspire her many readers and supporters."
Jill B. Smart, *Chief Human Resources Officer – Accenture*

"Have you thought of doing standup? You are that good."
Sandy Douglas, President, Coca-Cola.

"Fawn Germer has the uncanny ability to capture an audience at every touchpoint possible. She is smart, witty, charming, challenging, thought provoking, and engaging all at the same time. She is a remarkable speaker whose message remains with the audience long after the event has passed. Most important, she captures both the mind and the heart by inspiring men and women alike not just to go for the gold but to get it! I know. I went for it and I got it!"
Barbara Hartman , Vice President, Customer Business Development, Procter and Gamble

"Fawn has had a tremendous impact on my life. She gets right to what really matters. She touches an emotional chord that pushes us out of our comfort zones. Her real life stories help all of us to realize that our shortcomings can turn out to be our greatest gifts. She challenges us to take risks and pull ourselves to a level we never thought we dared to go."
Marie Quintana, *Vice President, Sales, PepsiCo*

"The sold out crowd of 457 people at the Ritz-Carlton gave you a rousing standing ovation because they were blown away by your moving, compassionate, uplifting presentation."
Richard (Dick) Lobo, President and CEO, WEDU

"WOW. Fawn is terrific, she absolutely understands the issues. More important, she knows how to truly connect with men and women to help them understand how to capture opportunities and challenge themselves. Fawn's realism comes across both as a speaker and author. She has lived her lessons and her honesty makes a difference." Kathy Hannan, *Managing Partner, KPMG*

"Fawn Germer's powerful points about taking initiative and overcoming obstacles are outstanding. Her down-to-earth style, personal experiences and sense of humor drive her message home." Paulo Costa, *fmr. CEO, Novartis*

"Fawn defines the word inspirational. I have heard her speak to audiences of +350 men and women and have them laugh, cry, get fired up, and leave determined to take a risk and dare to push their limits. She can pull this off because her own story is so inspirational and she really tells it from her heart. She really grabs you! Her books truly add dimension to her speaking engagements. I have read them all and enjoyed each one more than the last!" Maria Edelson, *VP of Sales for Evenflo*

"Fawn weaves a gripping personal tale into the leadership lesson and has everyone on the edge of their seats. She is warm, engaging, and builds lasting friendships from her associations. I highly recommend Fawn and would hire her again in a heartbeat." Robin Rodin, *Principle, The Rodin Group, fmr. Director of Leadership Development for GlaxoSmithKline*

"We hired Fawn as the keynote speaker for our annual meeting of healthcare market research professionals. As soon as she was onstage, she grabbed and held the attention of our 300+ attendees. She immediately connected with the audience by sharing the insights she's assembled from hundreds of interviews with successful men and women. She showed us that success and advancement will always be hard — it's hard for everyone– but with a passion to succeed and the courage to move the obstacle in front of us — or to go around it — we too can accomplish great things." Liz Coyle, *VP Global Business Planning & Commercial Operations at IMS Health*

"Fawn Germer stirs your soul. As you listen to her story and to the insights of the amazing people she has interviewed, you can easily internalize the message into your own life. She is easy to relate to because she is so real." *Kara Pelecky, Senior Manager of Infrastructure Projects, Exelon*

"Fawn is a wonderful author, speaker and friend who the Network of Executive Women considers one of its greatest supporters. We hired Fawn to write a book about the amazing women leaders of our industry-a real turning point for our organization- as we published it and sold over 15,000 copies! Fawn has been a key partner touring the country and facilitating panels of the women featured in the book at our various regional events... Fawn continues to be a source of inspiration, ideas and support for the Network-she embodies our ideals of diversity, inclusion, and finding one's voice." Alison Kenney Paul, *President, Network of Executive Women*

"She inspires others to take risks...To push their limits. To step out of their comfort zone... To achieve more than they might have thought possible... To be the best they can be."Maureen McGurl, *fmr. Executive Vice President. The Stop & Shop Supermarket Company*

"Fawn has the gift of finding the truth below the facts and telling it in ways that enable people to act. Because she is fearless and relentless she gets both the big picture and local action. She lives with the motto, 'Never let a crisis be wasted – in the crisis is an opportunity to grab'." Steffie Allen, *Principle, The Athena Group, LLC*

Best-selling Author ◇ International Speaker ◇ Four-time Pulitzer Nominee

FAWN GERMER

About the Author...

"If you want to read a very inspiring book, read *Hard Won Wisdom.*"

— *Oprah Winfrey"*

OK, the truth of it is, if you are a professional speaker and author, and Oprah Winfrey loved your book, you are going to use her quote. Over and over and over again, because Oprah doesn't feature very many books and if she has told the world how "very inspiring" you are, you'd better work it.

And maybe that really is the reason Fawn uses it. Or maybe it is because she once had a very nasty boss tell her that she'd never be more than she was at the time -- a newspaper reporter. In the decade since, Fawn has written best-selling books and become one of the nation's most beloved motivational speakers. Why? Because she's real. She's honest. And, she is the *only* author and speaker who has personally interviewed the most successful leaders of our times to learn their specific success and leadership strategies.

Her book, *Finding the UP in the Downturn,* shows how to stay in the game and *gain* ground at a time when everyone else is giving up. This continues Fawn's upbeat approach to success, showing how the only thing holding us back — is us.

Three years ago, she released *The NEW Woman Rules, which* was underwritten by the Network of Executive Women and includes interviews with nearly sixty of America's most powerful women in the corporate world today. Among them are many of the "Fortune 50 Most Powerful Women."

When Fawn left journalism to write her first book, it was rejected fifteen times -- by every major publisher in the country. She persevered, figured out the problem, then had her choice of publishers. She received her first copy of *Hard Won Wisdom* one day before the Sept. 11 tragedies, and had to get out there and promote her book -- and herself -- at a time of crisis. The experience taught her everything about obstacles, risk-taking and success. The book was buoyed by this four-time Pulitzer nominee's ability to connect so well with live audiences, and soon, thousands of people had connected to her powerful message of possibility.

As soon as Oprah told the world how inspiring Fawn's book was, Fawn became one of the nation's most sought after speakers.

Audiences love Fawn because she's been there. Up, down, winning and losing. Fawn shares stories of creating triumph out of defeat, inspiring others to believe in themselves and take the risks involved in living a bold life.

Fawn's second book, *Mustang Sallies,* hit best-seller lists within two weeks of its release. This ground-breaking book features interviews with more than 75 astounding trailblazers, including Hillary Clinton, Susan Sarandon, Janet Reno, Martina Navratilova, the late Ann Richards, Nadia Comaneci, Arianna Huffington, Carly Fiorina, Erin Brockovich and many, many others. The book looks at how women can find success by being themselves in a world where there is so much pressure to be like everybody else.

This acclaimed investigative reporter has worked as a Florida correspondent for both *The Washington Post and U.S. News and World Report.* Her distinguished reporting career earned her numerous state and national awards including four Pulitzer Prize nominations and the prestigious Green Eyeshade Award from the Society for Professional Journalists. She has worked as a staff writer for *The Miami Herald* and Denver's *Rocky Mountain News* and was an editor for *The Tampa Tribune.*

Fawn looks back on that old bully boss who tried to hold her back and says, "Some people have mentors. I had a tormentor." If not for him, she'd never have looked for anything different from her career. And, the one thing she has learned again and again is, it's all about the obstacles.

OFFICIAL WEBSITE:
www.fawngermer.com
DAILY BLOG:
www.hardwonwisdom.com
info@fawngermer.com
(727) 467-0202

No Other Speaker has Interviewed so Many of the Most Powerful Leaders in American Business

If you think hard work plus excellent performance puts you on the fast track, you're wrong. It puts you on no track at all.

Keynote star and best-selling author Fawn Germer went to the nation's most powerful corporate leaders to ask what it takes to take charge. She was told this: Performance is mandatory. But it is only one piece of what Fawn has identified as a three-pronged strategy that has been used to achieve stratospheric success.

Fawn's keynote presentations feature breakthrough insights gleaned from personal interviews with the CEOs of Fortune 500 companies — as well as the senior leaders who are positioned to take charge next .

From those interviews, the four-time Pulitzer-nominated journalist distilled success and leadership strategies that no other speaker can offer. Only Fawn Germer has gone to the CEOs, company presidents, CFOs, COOs, EVPs, and SVPs who have broken the barriers that hold us back. They told her exactly how they did it: what worked, and what didn't.

Oprah told the world that Fawn's writing is "very inspiring," and it is. Fawn is also one of the most entertaining speakers on the circuit today. After a recent keynote, Coca-Cola President Sandy Douglas asked her, "Have you thought of doing standup?"

Fawn's interviews resulted in new core rules for leadership and career success. Those rules are the cornerstones of her keynote presentations.

Speaking Information:
www.fawngermer.com
info@fawngermer.com
(727) 467-0202

CPSIA information can be obtained at www.ICGtesting.com
Printed in the USA
LVOW09s0901170414

381959LV00001B/94/P

9 780979 546631